SERVITUDE AND FREEDOM

Reading the Christian Tradition

Jonathan Dean

 EPWORTH

Scripture quotations are from the New Revised Standard
Version of the Bible, copyright 1989 by the Division of Christian
Education of the National Council of the Churches of Christ in
the USA. Used by permission. All rights reserved.

British Library Cataloguing in Publication data

A catalogue record for this book is available
from the British Library

978 0 7162 0654 5

This edition published 2009
by Epworth Press
Methodist Church House
25 Marylebone Road
London NW1 5JR

Typeset by Regent Typesetting, London
Printed and bound in Great Britain by
CPI Antony Rowe, Chippenham, Wiltshire

CONTENTS

History may be servitude,
History may be freedom.

T. S. Eliot, 'Little Gidding'
from the *Four Quartets*, 1944

INTRODUCTION

It may be that the idea for this book first came in early childhood. Visiting yet another stately home, cathedral or castle on the family holiday tour, I became increasingly intrigued by the past. What did it mean then? What difference does it make now? There is a piece of family folklore that describes my infant reaction to seeing Holbein's great depiction of Henry VIII, at Warwick Castle, observing his beard and assuming that, since he had one also, it must be a portrait of my father. In any case, I was hooked. The Tudor dynasty, in fact, never ceased to fascinate me, even into doctoral work and to the present day. Through the records of their lives, the figures of the past are almost as tangible as the buildings they inhabited, if slightly more unwilling to give up their secrets. The detective work has always inspired me, and it is in that lifelong fascination that these pages are rooted.

It is, however, necessary to say right at the outset what this book is *not*. It does not seek, for example, to be a thorough account of the course of Christian history. A number of those already exist, and are well done and readily to hand.[1] Nor does it claim to say the definitive word on any of the issues or historical questions discussed. The task of interpretation is always one undertaken in community, open to correction, revision and change. I aspire to some level of that humility in the reflections offered here. Third, there is no intent or effort to advocate any sort of historical fundamentalism. Sometimes, the tradition is

ix

at its best when it rejects the past: as we shall see. Historical theology has to do its work, not in splendid isolation, but in concert with other disciplines of mind and heart. Hopefully, it can inform them too.

Augustine once said of the Bible that it was possible either to paddle at the shoreline or wade far into its depths; the same is true, and perhaps more so, for the records of the last 2,000 years. Humanity's attempts to be faithful to a captivating itinerant preacher and rabbi from first-century Galilee, in times so utterly alien to his, are full of both triumph and disaster. It is the basic contention of this work, however, that those former efforts are important, indeed that they offer vital instruction and wisdom to us in our turn, and we ignore them at our peril. It can be daunting, faced with the sheer volume and variety of material telling us the story of our past, to know where to begin. The subtitle of the book, *Reading the Christian Tradition*, reflects my understanding that, primarily, an interpretative process is required if Christians are to feel connected to their Church's story in other generations. Augustine's comparison with the Bible thus seems doubly apt.

Part One, therefore, seeks to work through some of the questions and problems surrounding this interpretation. Chapter 1 looks at some basic, general questions about the value of historical awareness, and introduces some of the voices in contemporary culture that speak against its necessity. Chapter 2 is an attempt to describe the possibilities which being aware of and rooting ourselves specifically in our faith history can offer, and uses a range of images and understandings, including biblical ones, to do so. Chapter 3, finally, tries to put some flesh on these bones by offering an interpretative method for dealing with the stories, records and acts of the past. It makes no claims to offer much that is new: especially to those regularly used to reading, and trying to understand, the Bible. But it is my hope that, by applying some methods of biblical hermeneutics to reading our faith history, it too may become a little less remote, rather more accessible and a lot more relevant to us. The main contention of that chapter is that we need to start, simply by asking the right questions.

Part Two moves on to examine how some of this might 'cash out' in some current and pressing issues. Here, the author's preferences and interests are unashamedly indulged. Chapter 4 deals with questions of sexuality and the family, over which churches are splitting and Christians are fighting even at the time of writing. Chapter 5 looks at the thorny historical problem of religious violence, which never seemed more virulent than now, the long worldwide quest for justice and the emergence of 'green' theology in a time of impending global crisis. Finally, Chapter 6 is a study in the ways in which the Christian Church is striving to be faithful in a world of amazing diversity, both within and without its walls. As the world shrinks, and our security is challenged, how do we respond? In each case, a variety of voices is offered and evaluated, with the aim of fostering the understanding that we are not quite as alone as we sometimes think in this wonderful, promising and yet terrifying new century.

Here, too, there is not room for everything. In choosing to examine pressing issues of current debate and concern, there has not been space fully to consider those, perhaps more timeless, matters of theology and theodicy which always and everywhere affect and afflict humanity: the meaning of suffering, the inevitability of death and the life beyond it, the purpose and meaning of human life itself. On all of these, our tradition speaks richly and with the wisdom of experience across the span of time and place. They may call for a future volume. This book confines itself to method, and then to beginning to explore the ways in which past life may yet speak to present need, where the Church still divides, argues and threatens to self-destruct. It is there that we most need to begin.

Like all writers, I have incurred a huge number of debts too great to acknowledge adequately. Above all, however, I must thank my friend Martin Forward. He it was who steered me towards, and even nagged me into, historical research, who has unflaggingly encouraged me to teach and write, and who continues to be the wisest source of counsel, the most generous critic and the best kind of mentor and friend. There is no doubt in my mind that, without him, this book would never have been written. Scholars who are still fascinated by their subject, and who long to share it, have an infectious quality to them; Martin is one such, as is my doctoral supervisor, Eamon Duffy, whose influence and guidance have been immeasurable. While I want to thank him, I also feel the need to apologize for the weaknesses herein, onto which his laser-like mind would doubtless fasten. As authors always say when thanking their teachers: the errors contained in this book remain entirely my own. I am also profoundly thankful for those who have modelled for me the art (and necessity) of maintaining scholarly interests amid busy pastoral duties, and especially to Leslie Griffiths. My time at Wesley's Chapel increased my excitement at how past visions can inform present realities; Leslie's nurturing and support, then and afterwards, continue to mean a great deal. Natalie Watson played a crucial role in the genesis of this project. Her insistence that I offer something for publication and her help in shaping the proposal have been invaluable. I am truly grateful to her, and to her successor at Epworth, Angela Shier-Jones.

Some of the ideas and methods described here were first tried out in lectures, and on my 'Shaping of Christian Identity' class at Aurora University. I would like to thank those of them who stayed awake for their questions, insights and comments, which have certainly refined the end product. To and for Drew Taylor I am especially grateful. Other elements had their birth in the preparations for the Fernley Hartley lecture, given at the British Methodist Conference in July of 2007. Here, my thanks are due to Martin Wellings and his committee, both for the invitation to give the lecture and their help in making it happen. Stephen Burgess and Michael Townsend were on hand afterwards to offer wisdom, comment and liquid refreshment: and I thank them. Anne Brown, my District Chair, was always a wonderful pastor to me, and a wise counsellor. I owe her much.

I have written this book while serving a large United Methodist church in Downers Grove, a few miles west of Chicago. Without the kindness of friends there, the process of writing would have been far harder. Sue Devick generously gave me access to her historical library, and offered sources for Chapter 4. I must also and especially thank my wonderful ordained colleagues, the church staff for creating such a conducive environment for work of all kinds with their advice, assistance and hot beverages, and all those who've offered meals, encouragement, help and laughter. I have been truly blessed, in a strange and unfamiliar land, by new friendships. The 'sabbath' group, into whose company I am truly blessed to have been grafted, are a source of great delight, encouragement and ongoing vocational discernment. I treasure their love, generosity and wisdom, as well as Brian Erickson's invaluable 'kegerator'. In Illinois, I must thank David Aslesen, Betty Brunlieb, Anne and Chris Coon, Melissa Earley, Debbie Fisher, Lynn Higbee, Matt and Stacy Klepper, Kristen Larsen, James Preston, Debbie Rissing (who read an entire manuscript and offered hugely creative suggestions), Jeff Wasilevich: and Trey Hall, who, I hope, knows how important he has been to this project and how thankful I am for all he has offered in its creation. To these names, as always, I add those of my sister, Louise Norris, and Richard and Joy, my parents. I am constantly grateful for the love and prayerful support my family offers me, which in the case of the last three people named are very real and tangible even at a distance of 4,000 miles.

Finally, I have been more than usually conscious of my own debts to the past, my own inheritance of faith, in writing. I received from my grandparents gifts of many kinds while we shared this life. Something of my acknowledgement of that legacy is reflected several times in Part One. Since their deaths, I have continued to be acutely aware of their presence, guidance and love. I have also continued to be shaped, formed and guided by their faith, their varied insights and loves, and their wisdom. And I am grateful. It is to them – Ben and Florrie, Eddy and Hilda – that this book is dedicated, with the fondest memories, and the deepest love.

O Almighty God, who by the Holy Spirit hast made us one with thy saints in heaven and on earth: Grant that in our earthly pilgrimage we may ever be supported by this fellowship of love and prayer, and may know ourselves to be surrounded by their witness to thy power and mercy.
(Book of Common Prayer)

Advent 2008

Note

1 For example, Diarmaid MacCulloch, *Christian History: An Introduction to the Western Tradition* (2nd edn), Peterborough: Epworth, 2006.

Part One

INTERPRETING TRADITION

I

THE PROBLEM WITH THE PAST

Christians, like it or not, are a historical people. While their faith flourishes and gives meaning to life in the present, it is undeniably anchored in the past. It depends for its understanding on the lives, thought and example of those who have gone before; supremely, of course, on one man who went before, in Galilee about 2,000 years ago. When Christians come together in the most holy ritual they possess, they take bread and wine and remember him, hoping and praying that, somehow, doing so as a community will allow his life to be formed in theirs across the gap of centuries. Billions of Christians do this every week, because another man, Paul of Tarsus, told the Christians in Corinth a few years after Jesus' death that he had received as a 'tradition' the fact that Jesus ate such a meal with his disciples just before he died, and instructed them to keep his memory alive in the same way. Paul told them to preserve, practise and hand on the tradition of eating bread and drinking wine, so that Jesus would continue to live in them as they remembered him. It was, perhaps, the first tradition of the Christian Church, and the first of many. We are a historical people, a people of tradition. These days, however, it has become very important to be clear about what that means, and to understand the problems it poses for us in the present.

What do you think of when you hear the word 'tradition'?

What images come to mind? Perhaps the Jewish sense of customs and ideas which sustain a community by being passed on unchanged from one generation to the next: remember Tevye, in *Fiddler on the Roof*, singing with his fellow villagers of the durability and comfort of their life together, threatened with the incursion of a ruthless army and the destruction of their way of life. Or perhaps you may have a national custom in mind: the Trooping of the Colour, the May Day procession in Moscow, or the President of the US 'pardoning' the Thanksgiving turkey; often, these are occasions for pomp and circumstance which connect a nation to its past through ceremony or ritual. Literally, tradition means 'that which is handed on', as with Paul's story of the Last Supper. It comes from a Latin root which can have both good and bad meanings: one can be a 'traditor', or a 'hander-on', by treacherously turning one's friends into the authorities as well as by preserving for posterity a treasure of thought or belief.

In our churches and life together as Christians the word has more often assumed a pejorative meaning. If not quite as bad as treachery, being one who clings to tradition soon makes you a die-hard stick-in-the-mud, inflexible and unbending, refusing to countenance any change in the Church's life and stubbornly resisting all attempts to renew or alter any part of the Church's practice. Many people, clergy and lay, have encountered such people: those who are suspicious of innovations like dishwashers in the kitchen or overhead projectors in the sanctuary; those who find their sensibilities offended by communion wine served from a chalice instead of tiny glasses, or by the church meeting changing from its regular Tuesday evening slot to Sunday after worship. Suggest altering service times, or changing the character of Sunday worship, or starting a new youth group, or even some apparently trifling new idea, and the cry will quickly go up: 'It's not how we do things here. It's not our tradition'.

When churches come together, too, what is loosely termed 'tradition' swiftly becomes a stumbling block between them.

4

Not, let it be said, because of deep theological differences so much as because of the little practical changes like those already described which feel so alien and uncomfortable simply because they are unfamiliar. Here again, it's tradition which bears the blame for the slowness of ecumenical progress. Because of this innate human inertia and niggardliness, those who devote their lives and their efforts to ecumenical co-operation are often tempted to be critical of tradition itself. Their frustration gives rise to the widely held notion that it really doesn't matter what your 'tradition' is – Baptist, Roman Catholic, Presbyterian – because we're all Christians. While that's indisputably true, it has led to all manner of difficulty in the life and witness of the Church, as we shall discover. It confuses two different meanings of the word, and in the confusion we have often been tempted – and even persuaded – to throw the valuable baby of our rich history and developing self-understanding out with the grimy bath water of our trivial human obsessions.

Tradition, of course, has to do with history, but they are not exactly the same thing. History is both the record of the past and the way in which we study it. It involves the examination of the lives of those in previous generations and of the ways in which human existence has evolved and unfolded. Historians hope to be as faithful as they can to the sources they read from the time they are studying, and to make informed and insightful judgements about what was really going on. What motivated the people under consideration? What changed because of their actions, and why was the change significant? How was it consistent with the past, and how did it represent something entirely new?

Tradition is more complicated. It depends absolutely upon being historically informed, of course, but usually denotes or describes a movement, cause or way of thinking and believing within history: the trade unions, branches of music, philosophical 'schools', a religious faith. One writer has described it as 'the accumulated product of experiences that have long, continued usage'.[1] Often, we talk of a tradition in a more abbreviated, shorthand way than we can about the whole of history. In that come some of our difficulties with the word: if Methodist tradition is boiled down to communion wine in small glasses, we're in trouble; if the Anglican tradition is reduced to accommodation with any belief whatsoever, there are problems. Sometimes, traditions of all kinds discover that they have wandered into a cul-de-sac which is no longer true to their essential character, and they have to assess and regroup. We shall see several examples of that within Christianity later on. Suffice it to say that being faithful to a tradition means being willing to understand its breadth and to be prepared for the need to address its need for occasional revision. That's why history is so important for understanding a tradition. It keeps the record of origins, changes and development as a way of living and believing adapts to new circumstances. It tells our story, and the story still shapes us. It's put well by the person who said: 'Tradition is the living faith of the dead. Traditionalism is the dead faith of the living'.[2]

In this way, ever since the Church's inception, the witness of the lives of those who went before has been important, often vitally so, in determining how present-day Christians should respond to the circumstances in which they find themselves. In the first centuries of Christian life, from Paul onwards, there were great and drawn-out debates about exactly what Christians believed. Was Jesus human, divine or both? How was his divinity to be understood? What did it mean to understand God as having three distinct 'persons' in the experience of the believer? Which scriptural books were authentically Christian, and which were expressing dangerous or unhelpful sentiments? As the Church formed an opinion on these matters, a body of opinion grew up to which subsequent generations could look for guidance and wisdom. The Church's greatest scholars, leaders and saints left written and oral legacies behind them of their own insights and struggles. Always, however, there remained the question of how authoritative the past was to be thought to be. In the Roman Catholic Church, tradition came to assume an authority in the shaping of Christian doctrine and life almost equal to that of Scripture. Like any institution, the Church developed and evolved; and, like any institution, that evolution often seemed to take it far from its roots. The Church always maintained, though, that the process was faithful to the essential insights and priorities of the tradition of faith initiated by Jesus of Nazareth.

Over the course of the centuries, many have dissented from the formulation of that belief as defined by Rome. Most significantly, the Protestant Reformers of the sixteenth century[3] felt that the pendulum had swung too far in the direction of tradition. They argued and campaigned vigorously for a 'return' to the sole supremacy of the Bible, claiming that, in an excessive reliance on the modes and manners of Christian faith and practice that had evolved over the centuries, the Church had lost touch with first principles. But, in their own churches and societies, they soon found that the Bible was troublingly silent on some major issues – the precise formulation of the doctrine of the Trinity, the correct way to choose and ordain priests and ministers, the mode of church polity and governance preferred by God, the character of the Eucharist. Doing their best to rest their arguments on scriptural foundations, the Reformers nevertheless soon found themselves obliged to begin the invention of traditions of their own, as their churches grew increasingly separated from Rome. A parallel, Protestant, evolution of practice, organization and belief began.

Over time, two other elements that had always been talked about and described by Christian writers and thinkers began to assume a more definite and acknowledged place in the ongoing formulation of faith after the Reformation. Reason, the human ability to think and consider and exercise judgement, began more explicitly to be described as a necessary handmaid to the interpretation of Scripture and the reception and application of tradition. More controversially, so too did Experience, a word used to signify the human knowledge of and contact with the divine, the way in which Christians feel challenged to new expressions of mission in the world, which may not have a precedent in the Bible or in history to draw on. This so-called 'quadrilateral' became an increasingly common way for many Christians to think about the resources by which theology is done and Church life ordered. It also presents great challenges, in attempting to ensure that no one part of the structure is unduly privileged over another. Those challenges are at the heart of this consideration of how we are to think about the value and place of 'tradition' in the life of the Church today. Many leaders of renewal movements in the Church's history have actually made the claim to be rescuing the tradition from shame and misinterpretation, by listening to and being corrected by other voices within the very tradition that had gone awry. By what process can that happen? How much weight should tradition have when compared to the other resources for theology and the Christian life? In a world seemingly so different from previous ages and centuries, can our history of faith still teach us anything? If so, how, and what? With these questions in the air, it is important to begin our journey by understanding more deeply some of the reasons why the study of Christian history – and therefore the Christian tradition – is an often neglected and even maligned discipline in the contemporary Church.

Who do we think we are?

The notion that studying the past might shed light on the present and give hope for the future has come under critical and sometimes vitriolic pressure from all manner of sources, some of which are felt in the Church also. To begin with, great advances in science and technology from the Industrial Revolution onwards gave rise to the feeling that human progress was assured, that humanity in its advanced evolutionary condition was the master of its own fate and needed no help from primitive blueprints of the past. This industrial arrogance was neatly summed up by the famous observation of the great motor tycoon Henry Ford that 'all history is more or less bunk'. By the

1960s, the unfolding of history itself cast a dark shadow on that misplaced confidence, and prompted new thinking, still ironically rather hostile to history. The eminent Catholic scholar, Eamon Duffy, speaks of the way in which in that time there was a great deal of unease and upheaval in society: old ways of thinking were re-examined and re-evaluated; traditional values were questioned; what had previously seemed immovably fixed and set in stone was – to the outrage of some – fundamentally challenged. The permissive age of the 1960s and 1970s enabled much that renewed and liberated a whole generation. It also caused anything that smacked of being out of date, anything that appeared to emanate from a distant and irrelevant past, to be rejected. As, in the Roman Catholic Church, belief and practice from earlier generations were suddenly treated with suspicion, so in wider society, after the carnage and folly of two costly world wars, much wisdom from the past, much knowledge about the reasons why the world was as it was, was derisively dismissed as past its sell-by date.[4]

The repercussions of the great shifts of that period remain with us. The old ideas about human 'progress' seem to have been shattered by war, occupation, famine and genocide. An intense scepticism thus grows up about the very discipline of historical study itself, and some of this hostility also infects the way in which we think about history and tradition in the Church. The word usually used to describe the worldview prevalent behind all this is 'postmodern'. Postmodernity is notoriously difficult to grasp and encompasses a vast range of ideas and approaches to life and existence. Trying to define it is not unlike wrestling with a jelly. Very broadly and generally speaking, there is in postmodern thought an inbuilt hostility to historical ways of thinking and forming a sense of identity. Postmodernity resists any sense of what we might call a 'metanarrative', the notion of being a part of a human story of any kind with connections to and a direct line of descent from the past. Thus, some Christian ways of imagining the connection between the present generation and those of the past in

9

an unbroken line of belief and practice meet with derision in a postmodern age. It emphasizes that sense already described of rejecting the past as being an outmoded foundation upon which to build a present reality. It also tends to be extremely mistrusting about any claims about objective truth. As Professor Graham Ward describes it, postmodernity 'values ... ambivalence above certainty ... the fragment above the completed, surface rather than profundities'.[5]

Postmodernity has affected the Church, not just in a hostility towards historical study, but also in some of the ways in which Christians have started to think of their faith. Some have written of the experience of being 'post-Christian'; they redeploy images and metaphors central to Christian faith in order to shape their living, but downplay any abiding or lively connection to the historical figure of Jesus or to concrete historical moments in the life of the Church. Where movements of thought have attempted to reinstil into theology a connection with the Church's past, they have tended to do so by concentrating on specific figures or moments, and attempting to relate them to present concerns. The importance of the tradition remains undermined and downplayed. Postmodern people jettison a commitment to one particular faith tradition in favour of a more butterfly-like approach, choosing from many that which appeals to their subjective preferences and predilections, a tendency exemplified by the New Age movement. So too Christians find themselves uncertain about the place or value of their past. Dave Tomlinson, in his controversial book *The Post-Evangelical*, put it this way:

Is [postmodernity] good, bad, or indifferent from a Christian perspective? One thing is certain: it poses an entirely new interpretative situation for Christianity; and ... the evangelical church in the West is decidedly unprepared for the task of reinterpreting its faith. Why? Because it is lodged in a cultural time warp, still interpreting its faith in the language and ideas of the 'big story'. This is understandable: evangelicalism has had over a hundred years of dealings with the world of the big story. But it is time to move on.[6]

Attacks from outside: the trouble with tradition

More perhaps than in any other time or generation, religions in general and Christianity in particular have been the target of some fierce criticism in the late twentieth and early twenty-first centuries. As the world becomes smaller, through global communications and high-tech innovation, and as the distances between peoples and cultures diminish, religions are viewed much more as one identifiable phenomenon. The attacks on the USA in 2001 by Muslim extremists and the consequent fall-out, Israel's treatment of its Palestinian neighbours, the hardening of conservative positions in the Vatican, the sharp divisions within worldwide Anglicanism over sexuality and the fierce rhetoric of the Christian Right in the USA are among the factors that have hastened and worsened the criticisms levelled at religious people in general by those who themselves profess no traditional faith. One main thrust of their argument against religion is to point to history itself, not as a source of wisdom but rather as a damning record of the violent and repressive tendencies of religions and religious people, and as evidence of the need to abolish them, or at least curb their pernicious influence.

The British scientist Richard Dawkins is one of the more strident voices in this kind of polemical turning of the historical records on the faiths that gave rise to them. His book *The God Delusion* offered as a central plank of its thesis the centuries of violence and brutality which have arisen through the actions of religious people and even the teachings of religions themselves. The book in fact repeated many assertions that Dawkins had made in previous publications, but it attracted wide attention and was the focus of much commentary. In it, he points to inter-religious conflict and all manner of wars carried on in the name of religion, to the discrimination against women common throughout the history of most faiths, to the persecutions, torturings and inhumanity present in much religious life, and to the tendency of peoples of faith to use their beliefs to divide, exclude and oppress. Whatever the faults in the way Dawkins ascribes blame only to the influence of religion, while failing to address the deeper problem of the human condition itself, his work has fuelled the fires of those who see the history of faiths as purely negative. Whatever his failures truly to understand his subject, Dawkins has set hares running which many of his readers were only too willing to chase.

It will not do, however, simply to brush aside Dawkins' criticism without taking seriously the fact that the record of the Christian faith through the ages is often a dark and sinister one. Tradition cannot be mined as a rich resource of wisdom and truth unless there is also acknowledgement of its errors and failures, and even its wickedness. We cannot learn from the former and ignore the latter; but neither should we endlessly dwell on the latter while neglecting the former. Scientists like Dawkins must be all too aware of the darker side of their own potentialities and powers: weapons of mass destruction, eugenic mutilation, even the ability of new technologies to affect the economic and employment markets for ill as well as good. Similarly, people of faith can harness and interpret their faith traditions for good, only when they are properly mindful of the ways in which they have been turned to evil and used to diminish and divide others rather than allow them to flourish. Immersing ourselves more deeply in those failures, however, can be an exercise that turns us from our history in horror and disgust. It isn't hard to see why militant atheists like Dawkins use them that way.

For Christians, several particular events and a range of more general issues stand out as revealing the troubled and troubling side of their history. If they show the depths to which religious behaviour can sink, they demonstrate too the need to be aware of them in the present. The constant use by former President George W. Bush of the word 'crusade' is an obvious example.

Given that he used it almost exclusively in relation to his Middle East policy, it was little short of disastrous. Whether knowingly or not, he was invoking the bitter history of Christian Europe sending knights to the Holy Land in order to reconquer it for Christendom, in the course of which battles many thousands of Muslims were slain. Deep from the medieval past, the Crusades retain the power to shock and appal and to poison both relations with Muslims and the language of public and political discourse. Violence in all forms is a thorny legacy to handle, whether in warfare or persecutions such as the Inquisition and the Reformation disputes. A later chapter discusses it in more depth; suffice it to say for now that we ignore its lasting effects at the cost of our integrity and authority to speak to the contemporary world.

Related to that is the Church's complicity in injustice and suffering through the centuries of its existence. Until the eighteenth century, indeed, the Church generally condoned the trade in and possession of slaves. It had a good, and even a scriptural, mandate to do so. So, how was it that scripturally faithful and historically educated men like William Wilberforce and John Wesley came to see slavery as a practice that stood diametrically opposed to the gospel and a shocking and brutal judgement, not just on the Church but on humanity in general? Again, being faithful to tradition entails not merely accepting uncritically the pronouncements of religious leaders, but taking seriously what it means to face up to the wickedness which has unthinkingly been absorbed into our life. Such difficult work lay behind the work of the Second Vatican Council in the 1960s, which we shall examine in the next chapter; the unimaginable horrors of the Shoah[7] and the death of several million Jews in Nazi gas chambers made the task unavoidable, however gruesome and unwelcome it felt to those involved. And it is not difficult to see why being 'up close and personal' with this kind of history leads some to think that it should not be attempted, or that religion must necessarily be bad.

Later chapters will also seek to deal with rather more generalized and long-lasting issues within the Christian tradition which are frequently cited in its prosecution. The marginalization of women within the Church would be one obvious category. How are we to understand the process by which many of the world's churches now ordain women to the priesthood and the episcopacy, and the understanding which informs them that this is not unfaithful to the tradition? How are we to understand the fact that women were so sidelined for so long? In an institution that is supposed to be about transformation, about not blindly following societal norms but rather being the catalyst for change, what can we learn about the Church's historical failure to be true to its prophetic roots? One answer to the question is to know the tradition better, rather than dismissing it as failed. A knowledge of the various and influential (though rarely central) roles played by women in the Church's life and thought helps us to acknowledge a vital though often hidden contribution that was quietly being offered. A deeper attention too to the ways in which the Church has dealt with the complexities of human sexuality over the course of time might help the contemporary internecine strife around the problem. In each case, it may be possible to tease out strands of the tradition, to understand that it works, not as a single melodic line but as a rich and complex harmony of voices.

Standing in a large room

How, then, should Christians view their tradition? When our culture and society resist its importance, when those outside the Church force us to face our own past failures in order to rub our noses in our religious heritage and its attendant horrors, what is our response? Even those within the Church sometimes doubt the ability of history to inform our present situation. This was written by an eminent New Testament scholar in the mid-1980s and sums up the position well, if alarmingly:

[Jesus'] message was for the present, in view of an over-whelmingly dominant future ... What mattered about Jesus was not what he inherited but what he initiated ... The distinctive mark of Christianity, that which gave it the impetus to be a new faith, was, as Paul (partly) perceived, its concern with present and future. From that point of view, the constant turning to the past, whether Jewish or ecclesiastical, for authorities rather than for landmarks, is a profoundly distorting change of front. The concern with present and future might be characterized as resulting from a simplicity of trust in God, a sense of his immediacy, and a readiness to accept the here and now as his and as the scene on which he must be met and served.[8]

The author missed entirely, despite his biblical learning, the very explicit ways in which the New Testament roots its message in a faithfulness to the past; what God was doing in Christ represented, the New Testament authors tell us, the new covenant promised to the prophets, the widening of Israel's influence envisaged by the great seers of the Hebrew Scriptures. It is arguable that the whole New Testament is trying to make that point and draw those links! But he articulates a commonly held view, that creative and imaginative responses to present needs for the sake of shaping the future are not to be found in losing oneself in the past. Perhaps at this point it would therefore be timely to begin to think about an appropriate model to use when understanding the role of tradition.

It may be helpful to remember the old and now rather tired and outdated discussions about 'law' and 'grace' in the Bible. Some people imagine tradition to be Law: fixed, unbending, allowing no room for change or growth because it straitjackets us into a pattern, a rigid cage from which there can be no deviation. Indeed, the Church sometimes reinforces this misconception, by showing itself to the world to be entirely unwilling to enter genuine, open dialogue on certain subjects, and refusing to accept the reality of people's lives, constrained by dogma and the inflexibility of historical precedent. To take one example, the Christian Right in the USA will apparently endorse any presidential candidate, no matter what their own circumstances or previous record, as long as they take the 'correct' stance on three major issues: abortion, marriage and gay rights (or lack thereof). During the 2008 Presidential primary race, the leaders of that movement slowly accommodated themselves to Mitt Romney, the only leading candidate for President to share their views on social policy and the obstacle of whose Mormonism – which they had previously seen as heresy – they learned to overcome. When asked, such leaders always respond by pointing to the record of Scripture and the unchanging stance of the Church down the ages. No matter that, in many other areas, they themselves have seen fit to do away with both Scripture and the past witness of the Church. They do not seek legislation to make divorce impossible, despite the clear line on that issue over the years; they do not fight against capital punishment, despite all their own rhetoric on the 'sanctity of life'. They do make the disaster of regarding the tradition as 'law' all too clear. Others regard the refusal of Pope Benedict XVI to consider the ordination of women or the ordination even of celibate homosexuals as a similar mistake, and one in which he has demonstrated his lack of the understanding and courage that distinguished many of his predecessors.

In some cases, Christians present a false and misleading notion of tradition as being immutably fixed around the cult of personality or an individual. The nineteenth-century Pope Pius IX presided over the First Vatican Council, a large part of whose deliberations concerned the issue of the pope's authority to define and declare doctrine for the whole Church. Having kept his counsel for many days, he finally exploded, and showed his hand, when one of his cardinals described the pope and bishops as 'the witnesses of tradition'. Pius's forthright reply was to exclaim: '*I* am the tradition!' The Council did not entirely concur. Roman Catholicism is by no means alone in the danger of viewing tradition this way, however. For all branches of the faith which originated through the witness and ministry of a single individual, there are always difficult questions to answer about how their legacy is best to be received and shaped for the present. Methodists often struggle to liberate John Wesley's unique contribution to Christianity from his eighteenth-century context or else try to live there themselves thinking that thus they honour the denomination he initiated. Salvationists only recently allowed the Victorian uniforms of William and Catherine Booth to be somewhat updated in order to present a slightly less austere face to the world. Anglicans who cling to Archbishop Thomas Cranmer as the standard-bearer for an unchanging language of liturgy and a 'high church' view of the sacraments are perhaps most to be pitied, in their failure to understand how radical – and how thoroughly Protestant – his work was, however it appears to twenty-first-century eyes and ears.

The United States of America offers an interesting secular illustration of this kind of problem. As the founding principles of the nation were being established in the eighteenth century, it was thought expedient to draw up a constitution, which would define the shape of government but also delineate some fundamental values and core beliefs of the new country. Some of that, of course, was shaped in reaction against the British colonial authority so recently rejected. Britain's constitution-free and rather messy political structures and retention of a hereditary monarchy were certainly defining factors in shaping a brave new land that represented an Enlightenment exercise in statecraft. The American Constitution was ratified in 1788 and augmented by the ten amendments of the Bill of Rights three years later. From that time, it has defined, limited and set the parameters for everything which can be legally done in the USA. The Supreme Court ultimately rules on whether laws, actions or proposals, at both state and federal level, are 'constitutional' and therefore within the boundaries of acceptability envisaged by the founding fathers. The whole exercise is about nothing so much as inheriting and interpreting a tradition.

With the Declaration of Independence, the Constitution remains one of history's most profound and eloquent statements of the high ideals of representative democracy and enlightened government.

It also, naturally, causes huge problems. It can be extraordinarily difficult and often impossible to imagine how previous generations would have reacted to situations far removed from and utterly unlike anything in their experience. When the mind of a previous generation still defines a nation in the present day, the arguments over interpretation and application of the Constitution are not hard to foresee. The Supreme Court has to function as the final and unchallengeable (except by another Supreme Court decision) authority on the question: the referees' decision is final, binding even on the President, who yet retains the power of nomination to its bench. Thus, great political debates always attend upon the appointment of new Supreme Court justices, and the candidates' intentions and interpretations of the Constitution attract detailed scrutiny: these interpretations can change history. The struggles for the full integration of African Americans and for the equality of women were – and are still – fought on the basis that the Constitution's basic principles, that 'all men are created equal' were not being observed, even at the time of its creation. In 2008, the Supreme Court was required to revisit the Second Amendment, which guarantees the right to bear arms to American citizens. Some argue that its provision is clearly and solely an eighteenth-century one: for small towns to be able to form a militia in self-defence against those who would threaten their freedom or integrity. It therefore has nothing to do with the right of an individual living in suburban Chicago or in an apartment in downtown Memphis to carry a rifle or keep a pistol in the bedside drawer: or that of a Vice President indiscriminately to shoot his friends in the forest. Others insist that the law protects freedoms and should be taken at face value, and thus requires no reinterpretation for the present, even in the light of soaring gun crime figures. This 'constructionist' reading, when taken to its extreme, foresees no modern circumstances under which the terms of the Constitution may find latitude for adjustment. It is hard to see how this view would work in a modern society, in fact: but there are those who espouse it, many of them Christians.

By contrast, imagining the Christian history we inherit as a grace-giving framework in which to 'live and move and have our being' offers the notion that we do not simply have to abide slavishly by the mind and thought of a previous generation remote from our own. The people of each place and time have to try to be faithful, not just to their belief systems, but also to the context in which they practise belief, and attempt to discern what it means to be the Church where they are. Seeing tradition this way requires us not just to adopt an inappropriate and ill-fitting set of clothes from the past; it allows us to cut the cloth for ourselves from the wealth of material which people of great faith, wisdom and insight have handed down to us. It also makes it far more complicated to assimilate the value of our history for ourselves, since the exercise is clearly a creative one, requiring not just obedience but also openness, integrity and the willingness to be patient, attentive and even wrong. In Chapter 3, we shall think about some of the ways in which we might envision this process, with all its attendant complications. In any case, it is certainly preferable to viewing the Christian tradition as a cruel master, unchanging, unbending and without remorse. As Rabbi Mordecai Kaplan wisely observed, the past has a vote – but not a veto.

The rise in the interest we are taking in tracing our family histories may help to provide a clue about how to understand our faith history. Television programmes such as *Who Do You Think You Are?* have tapped into the increasing fascination with finding out about family trees which has been evident in recent years. It is interesting to ask what we think we are discovering in pursuing such research. Certainly, it is not that we shall find distant relatives whose lives we may copy in every detail in order that our own may be enriched; rather, it is to fulfil a curiosity about where we 'came from' as a means to helping us to understand how we came to be where we are, and how our life fits into the wider story of that of our human family. In my own case, I was fortunate to have close relationships with both my grandfathers when a child and teenager. I learned much from each of them, and know that my own outlook, values and character have been moulded immeasurably by their influence and example. While my life is both shaped and continually informed by theirs, however, it is in many ways far removed from the realities they inhabited. In order to mine the riches of their example to me, the legacy they leave me, I do not feel that I have to mimic them by being an agricultural labourer, local preacher, plumber or church choirmaster. They would have been horrified if I had!

In the same way, when we speak of tradition as a foundation block of the Christian faith, we do not speak of something that is a set of rules to be followed, or a brutal monolith that never changes. We speak rather of something both more intricate and more difficult to fathom. We speak of what the Psalmist sings of, at least as beautifully mistranslated by the King James Bible, in having a sense of the rich inheritance we receive from the countless faithful lives and witnesses that have preceded ours: 'Thou hast set my feet in a large room' (Psalm 31.8). Eamon Duffy pursues this image of the tradition, comparing the fullness of what we receive from previous generations to a large and old church, which shows evidence of additions and accretions over many centuries, and yet which speaks in a multitude of voices to us in a variety of ways.[9] Having grown up in the small cathedral city of Ely, I find the idea rich and meaningful. Whenever I entered the cathedral, and to this day, I have a deep and holy sense of the way in which it has been 'prayed in' over many centuries by millions of people, from its founder St Etheldreda in 673, through medieval monks to seventeenth-century soldiers in the Civil War, to all those who visit it at the present time. From the massive ancient Norman arches, to the Victorian painted ceiling, the modern artwork and the making of music from across the ages, there is something in its structure, furnishing and worshipping life which speaks differently to me, depending on my mood, on the day, and particular circumstances of my life at the time. The lofty grandeur of the lantern tower and the intimate beauty of Bishop West's chantry offer contrasting yet equally instructive places to meditate on the character of God. The desecration of the Lady Chapel bears silent witness to the destructive forces of religious iconoclasm which have also marked the place and its people. Truly, this is a 'large room' in which to give God thanks for variety, and the changes of the passing ages. It's a place in which the voice of God is heard in a range of ways: breath-taking, challenging, comforting, warning, uplifting, renewing and giving peace. Our faith history is such a space too.

The chapters that follow aim to explore a few of the spaces in this large room. To begin with, some general reflections on how best to appreciate the architecture and understand its evolution, and then some specific attempts to tackle particular and perhaps difficult features and to see whether tradition might be able to liberate contemporary Christians, and not enslave them, as they wrestle with them. The aim of all this, too, might not be so very different from visiting a large, historic house of prayer. In discovering our tradition and considering how to apply it, we are reminded of our own place and significance in the movement of the ages and the purposes of God; we are given a sense of a community, those whose example we follow, from whose mistakes we learn, and whose prayers sustain us in our exploration; we are enriched, challenged, renewed and given pause for thought. In giving attention to the witness of those who go before us, our own witness is held up to scrutiny and refinement. We emerge into the crisp air of our own times with just a little more insight into the resources of faith, reason and hope which they exhibited and which might inform us too. The seventeenth-century priest and poet George Herbert used the image of international trade to write of this necessity of communication and conversation between the ages; in doing so, he perfectly captured the twin dangers we face, in needing to be neither so arrogant as to dismiss the testimony of the past, nor so shallow as to doubt the importance of the contribution of our own generation:

> God in all ages hath had his servants to whom he has revealed his truth ... and as one country doth not bear all things that there may be a commerce, so neither hath God opened or will open all to one, that there may be a traffic in knowledge between the servants of God for the planting both of love and humility.[10]

Notes

1 F. H. Thompsett, *Living with History*, Cambridge: Cowley, 1999, p. 11.

2 The verdict of the religious historian Jaroslav Pelikan, in an interview for *U.S. News & World Report*, 26 July 1989.

3 Given that this is a book about Christian history, there is no need to refer to 'CE' (or 'AD') when naming centuries. When dates cited are before Christ, I use the suffix 'BCE'.

4 Eamon Duffy, *Faith of Our Fathers*, London: Continuum, 2004, p. viii.

5 Graham Ward, 'Postmodern Theology', *Christianity: The Complete Guide*, London: Continuum, 2005, pp. 956–7.

6 Dave Tomlinson, *The Post-Evangelical*, London: Triangle, 1995, pp. 78–9.

7 'Shoah' is now the preferable term for the Nazi destruction of European Jewry; its meaning, 'devastation', is much more accurate than that of the older 'Holocaust' ('sacrifice') which imposes a false interpretation on unimaginable horror, brutality and murder.

8 Leslie Houlden, *Connections*, London: SCM Press, 1986, pp. 121–2.

9 Duffy, *Faith of Our Fathers*; pp. 168–87.

10 George Herbert, *The Complete English Poems*, London: Penguin, 1991, p. 205.

2

THE POTENCY OF TIME

How Tradition Gives Life

Remembering Grandma: our family history

Christmas, they say, is a time for family. Growing up, I experienced big family Christmases at home, and was fortunate
that my grandparents lived close by and could share in the cele-
bration with us. It led to some memorable moments, of the
kind that all families experience: jokes that fell flat, misunderstandings that persisted all afternoon in frosty silence, gifts that
weren't quite what we children had hoped for, occasions in
which some of us saw the funny side and chuckled the rest of
the day and, above all, the sheer joy of being together, of taking time for company and relaxation, of watching *The Sound
of Music* together and singing along, of having that deep and
wonderful sense of being with people who love you and take
you as you are, in whose presence you can simply be yourself.
I cherished that, and still do.

My grandparents are no longer alive, and so family Christmases, when we all manage to be together, are rather quieter.
The interesting thing is that they're still enriched in some way
by the presence of loved ones who've died. Every Christmas
we think of grandma, who needed to start her long, slow journey to the dining table about ten minutes before the sprouts
were ready, and smile; we remember too that she would still

be eating long after the rest of us finished, and chuckle; we call grandad to mind, rather deaf and always so polite about asking for the subtitles on the television for the afternoon film. And, as we remember, and laugh, and smile, and fondly recall them, it is as though they were there. Something essentially good and true about them and the life we shared with them lives on, in our family Christmas, into the present. Their influence on us, the ways in which they have shaped us and changed us, are indelible and precious and eternal. I think it's true to say that we can often sense this growth and enrichment too, even when we remember the more difficult years, as they aged, and grew more frail, and times when the atmosphere occasionally grew strained. We learned something of truth and goodness, even in that, by God's grace. As Frederick Buechner writes, 'when you remember me, it means that you have carried something of who I am with you, that I have left some mark of who I am on who you are. It means that you can summon me back to your mind even though countless years and miles may stand between us.'[1]

I wouldn't forget my grandparents for anything. If I did, my life would be immeasurably poorer. What happens at family Christmases, furthermore, is somewhat similar to what is happening when Christians remember their past. Not everything they call to mind will be edifying, or easy, or comfortable; but forgetting altogether would be far worse. Forgetting altogether would mean losing touch with influences which have shaped them, and experiences which have given insight and life, and enabled growth. It would also disconnect them from the very life lessons from which they could learn. Amnesia in groups and institutions is as tragic and destructive as that experienced by individuals, and teaches us to beware the kinds of voices in our culture which undermine or reject the value of the past. It's a terrifying experience, temporarily to lose your memory. You lose the anchors you have on who you are, and what structure your life has, and where you are supposed to be going. Anyone who has ever had to live with a period of memory loss bears witness to the anxiety, loneliness and isolation of it all, and the fear that you may never get your bearings again. To *choose* amnesia for yourself would be extraordinary. That's why traditions of faith should guard against the temptation too.

I used to lead services occasionally in a wonderful Methodist home, specifically caring for those with dementia. Those few experiences and my time there swiftly taught me that memory loss is painful, laden with grief and hard to bear with dignity or grace. It also taught me that choosing not to keep a memory is folly. The residents at Westbury were fortunate to be the recipients of expert and tender care from professionals who understood their disease and who made their lives as dignified and meaningful as they possibly could. Even so, the quality of their care could not disguise the tragedy of the slow unravelling of their memories. People who once taught in schools or ran their own businesses could no longer recognize their children; those who formerly crafted poetry or painted pictures could not so much as write their names. For those closest to them, perhaps, the pain was worst. One of my colleagues, who was the chaplain there and had many years of experience with spiritual care of dementia patients, used to call what they went through a 'long goodbye'. It was a drawn-out, agonizing loss of identity: and it cut to the heart anyone observing it and its effect on families and loved ones. It's not too exaggerated, nor does it belittle that experience, to suggest that Christians choose this kind of tragedy, and such a loss of identity, when they turn their backs on their past.

Just as the memory of family life gives us a sense of our place within it and of the ways in which our membership of a family has shaped us, so our collective memory about a tradition to which we belong should inform our place within the human family throughout time. Indeed, trying to ignore the influence of our families upon us is as foolish as trying to ignore our human history; it doesn't alter who we are, but rather simply leaves us ignorant about why we are that way. Fans of great literary epics which chart the life of a family over several generations identify with this principle. John Galsworthy's *Forsyte Saga* is a case in point. June is initially estranged from her father Jolyon because of his desertion of her mother when she was a baby; and though they are subsequently reconciled, it profoundly affects their relationship. In turn, his son, young Jolyon, inherits the family hatreds which turn his engagement into a cause for suspicion, fear and ultimately death. The players are constrained and surrounded by the actions and judgements of previous generations, and mere ignorance of how and why this happens does not prevent it from happening anyway. The consulting rooms of therapists and counsellors are daily full of those of us who need to go through the sometimes painful process of working through our early life and the effects of family behaviour in order to make sense of our present and face the future.

Human societies and traditions, no less than individuals, must both grapple with the family mistakes that still constrict them, and receive the inheritance of past glories, the 'family silver' so to speak, in order fully to understand themselves. This will not impose a solution or a way of proceeding on them for the future, but it is necessary in order to create a framework in which informed, wise, faithful choices for the future are possible. Remember Rabbi Mordecai Kaplan again: it's important to give the past a voice but not a veto. An amnesiac institution, of any kind, is no more free to choose a new future than an amnesiac individual: simply more likely to do itself and others harm by forgetting the basic principles of life and losing its grip on its own identity. The ancient Roman statesman Cicero liked to point out that ignorance of the past results in permanent childhood. In many ways, a kind of renewed and tragic childhood is often the result of amnesia of all kinds.

It is not just religious people who need or understand this sense of the 'family' to which they are connected through time. Historians of all kinds are arrogant enough to think that they might be doing others a favour by offering the stories and insights of the past to the needs of the present. One of them, Martin Marty, puts it this way: 'we study history in order to intervene in history'.[2] Perhaps we see this in the world of politics too. All politicians look to certain 'heroes' of the past, men and women who understood how to gain office, and, most of all, use it wisely once they had it. Those who really changed society, or even the nation, whose policies made a lasting impact, are frequently cited and held up by those seeking to follow them: Winston Churchill, Clement Attlee, Franklin Delano Roosevelt, Nelson Mandela. It was said of Tony Blair early in his leadership of the Labour Party that he devoured political biographies, eager to learn from the lives and careers of his predecessors in office how to wield power and understand statecraft. It will be the task of future historians and posterity to judge how well he learned. The point is that, however new and unprecedented the particular circumstances facing a leader, there are always lessons of character and judgement which can be learned from the figures of the past. There is a family principle of some sort at work, and memory of *all* the families of which we are a part is important.

Scientists, too, usually understand that they are a part of a 'family' of people with an insatiable curiosity to know more and understand better the way the universe fits and holds together. The discoveries of each successive age cannot help but build on those of the previous ones. Modern astronomy traces a direct line back to Galileo; atomic physics still relies on Einstein; medical research cannot do without the influences and legacy of Curie, Fleming, Pasteur and Lister. Scientists have to wrestle, too, with the appalling destructive capabilities they have unleashed and can never 'uninvent', a realization which made Alfred Nobel, the inventor of dynamite, also the initiator of an international prize for peace. There is simply no way in which scientists can choose amnesia or ignore their family history. It has made them at one and the same time into healers, with a cure for cancer within their grasp, and, in the words of Robert Oppenheimer, a creator of the atomic bomb, 'the destroyers of worlds'.[3]

Sir Isaac Newton, the famous seventeenth-century British scientist, understood this very well. He quoted the twelfth-century scholar John of Salisbury, who reminded his students that all knowledge and insight was gained only 'by standing on the shoulders of giants'.[4] In other words, by drawing on the work and witness of those who went before us, we fashion our response to our times: but we cannot and do not do that in a vacuum. So insightful was his comment thought to be, about the way in which the human family must understand itself, that the quotation appears on the British two-pound coin and as the motto for the Google Scholar search engine! The best-known scientist of the present age, Stephen Hawking, compiled a collection of the most important writings of the greatest scientists of history, and invoked Newton's comment in entitling it *On the Shoulders of Giants*. Christians who would treat the inheritance and legacy of their faith family lightly or contemptuously could look to scientists – or even to politicians! – to gain a better understanding of how life-giving and essential the reception of a tradition can be.

There is a very similar lesson to be learned in the arts as well. It would be hard to imagine anyone trying to sit down and write a play without any knowledge whatsoever of the ancient Greek playwrights, or Shakespeare, or for anyone to attempt poetry without ever having had experience of how others before them went about the task. Artists and painters too find their own uniqueness and individual expression by building on – or even reacting against – those who went before. Leonardo da Vinci thought knowledge of the past was a 'nourishment' to the artistic mind; addressing the Royal Academy of Art in 1953, Winston Churchill reflected that 'without tradition, art is a flock of sheep without a shepherd'. He reminded his hearers of the limits of tradition too by adding, 'without innovation, it is a corpse'. Writing this, my first book, I am constantly recalling the examples of other books I have read, and those whose style and use of language I have admired. For all that, it's still my book, not theirs. In *The Tempest*, Shakespeare put it well in the mouth of Antonio:

... what's past is prologue, what to come,
In your and my discharge.[5]

As with painting and writing, so with music. The composer
Benjamin Britten once criticized a fellow musician for writing
an opera in total ignorance of how others had done so before,
and ending up, in his view, with a muddled and confusing cac-
ophony. He likened the process to map-reading: there may be
many ways of getting where you want to be, but it's sensible
at least to discover how others have gone before you, before
setting out into the dark without a guide of any sort. So it was
that Johannes Brahms, in the nineteenth century, sweated and
laboured long and hard before attempting to write a symphony
after Beethoven, conscious of the mantle he would thereby inherit and the weight of the foregoing tradition. So it was, later
in the century, that the young Edward Elgar fled to his beloved
Malvern Hills, armed only with the scores of Beethoven and
Brahms as he attempted to steep himself in the art form to which
he wished to devote himself. Twentieth-century movements of
imitation and homage to previous generations of composers
illustrate the creative and inspirational power of tradition too,
at least in the hands of the greatest. Francis Poulenc's 1928
Concert Champêtre is written for harpsichord and orchestra,
and is a salute to the form and style of the seventeenth century.
In character, melody and unmistakable insouciance, though, it
could only be by Poulenc.

For Christians, however, the story of their family history
has, by their own claim, a different element to it. That is, it isn't
simply a useful and educative collection of tales about ancestors, nor merely a way of understanding how we come to be as
we are, and why we find ourselves both constricted and freed
by the inheritance we receive from the past, important though
those things are. It is also – and perhaps primarily – *the story
of God's dealings with God's people over time*. In other words,
for all the tragedies, misunderstandings and sheer wickedness
of our Christian history, it contains, we think, a deeper, truer,

more hopeful story: that God has not finished with us, and that, through the changes and disturbances and questions of each passing age, God keeps faith with us. However different the periods of time that we examine, there should be a continuity of some sort to it, the continuity of the presence, love, guidance and grace of God, however ignored, marginalized, unheard or misrepresented those things are. It is at some level, perhaps, possible to have a conversation across the span of ages with those who have gone before us and find that some thread of continuity exists between their faith and ours. We are all members of Christ's body. As Archbishop Rowan Williams says, if that is really our hope and expectation, then 'historical understanding is not a luxury in such a context'.[6] As we begin to try and tease out how we are to have that conversation with family members so far away from us and so different from us, to assess our inheritance and understand our formation and identity as history has shaped them, we should begin by seeing how our earliest faith ancestors thought of what had gone before them. In other words, we should look to how the biblical authors understood the past.

Explaining the Stones: biblical calls to remember

The need to recall the past in order to shape the future with faithfulness to God's call saturates the Old Testament. The book of Deuteronomy was written as Moses' final instructions to the people of Israel before his death and their crossing into Canaan, the promised land which flowed with milk and honey. Right before they receive this inheritance from God's hand, Moses reminds them of the main principles of the Law, and especially that they should love God with all their heart, soul, mind and strength. Supremely, in their future life together as the chosen people, the story of God's goodness to them should guide their responses and form the foundations of their identity and self-awareness:

When your children ask you in time to come, 'What is the meaning of the decrees and the statutes and the ordinances that the LORD our God has commanded you?', then you shall say to your children, 'We were Pharaoh's slaves in Egypt, but the LORD brought us out of Egypt with a mighty hand ... He brought us out from there in order to bring us in, to give us the land that he promised.'
(Deuteronomy 6.20–23)

Similarly, the Law frequently urges compassion towards those dispossessed, downtrodden and oppressed, pleading with the Israelites to recall: 'you yourselves were once slaves in Egypt'. The memory of their past and of God's faithfulness is to be a controlling one, which governs their outlook and their reactions to their neighbours. So too is their connection to the great figures of faith in the distant mists of time, those who by their unquestioning obedience and extraordinary courage in trusting God overcame some fairly deep human flaws to become saints. The people's God is indeed the God of Abraham, Isaac and Jacob.

The writer of the book of Joshua continued the idea, in describing the people finally crossing into their new homeland. As momentous in its way as the crossing of the Red Sea, this story too features a miraculous intervention that leaves the waters of the River Jordan dammed, allowing the people easy entrance into Canaan. Once they have passed over, Joshua, the new leader of Israel, orders twelve stones to be laid at the camp that night, a sign and reminder of the remarkable events of an extraordinary day. Again, the command to be a people concerned with the past, a people concerned with 'handing on' the tradition, comes to the fore in Joshua's instructions:

When your children ask in time to come, 'What do those stones mean to you?', then you shall tell them that the waters of the Jordan were cut off in front of the ark of the covenant of the LORD. When it crossed over the Jordan, the waters of

the Jordan were cut off. So these stones shall be to the Israelites a memorial for ever.
(Joshua 4.6–7)

What follows this event in the Old Testament is a succession
of books, containing a detailed history of the ongoing life of
Israel: prophets, kings, enemies, victories and defeats, highs
and lows, judgements both good and bad and their effect on
the nation and its relationship with God. Throughout, there
is still that clear purpose from Moses' final instructions to the
people and before: that it is by measuring their life against
God's past goodness and generosity that their fidelity to the
covenant will be judged. Further, only a historical understanding will allow the people fully to grasp the extraordinary fidelity and goodness of God, through all their turbulence and
disobedience.

The kings and prophets also demonstrate the importance of
memory in the eyes of the biblical authors. For all his very
human failings, King David became the standard by which subsequent Israelite kings were judged. His own son and successor, Solomon, brought about the ignominious division of his
father's kingdom because he himself had not been faithful to
his father's example. 'His heart was not true to the LORD his
God', says the books of Kings, 'as was the heart of his father
David' (1 Kings 11.4). The continuing presence of David's descendants as rulers over one of Israel's tribes was a testimony
to God's love of David and his place as the founder of the
dynasty; the remaining ten tribes were handed over to Solomon's servant Jeroboam, with the instruction:

If you will listen to all that I command you, walk in my ways
and do what is right in my sight ... as my servant David did,
I will be with you, and will build you an enduring house, as
I built for David, and I will give Israel to you.
(1 Kings 11.38)

The people of Israel (and Judah) were unlikely ever to lose entirely a historical perspective, daily reminded by the division of their country both of the integrity and the folly of their former kings. King David himself remained for many centuries – and even to the present day – the model of kingship, a historical example to look to: someone who, through a deep and passionate humanity which often led to hurt and sin, also managed to shape a nation in righteousness, justice and covenant faithfulness.

As things began to unravel for Israel, as enemies from the north and east pushed closer and threatened their security and independence, increasingly a group of holy men and women collectively known as the prophets emerged and fashioned a unique response to events. The prophets, whose public ministries span the period from the eighth century before Christ until the composition of the book of Daniel in the second century BCE, relied themselves on a historical perspective to undergird their message and underscore their emphases. They pointed to the covenant, and Israel's forgetfulness of it; they dwelt on God's goodness to the people in the past as evidence of God's desire to be good in the present; they spoke of David, of Moses, and of significant historical events in order to shed new light on Israel's troubled situation. God was not so much rejecting Israel, they claimed, as allowing Israel to feel the effects and consequences of her folly and infidelity. Instead of wringing their hands and indulging in self-pity at their fate, instead of questioning the character of the God who had allowed their enemies literally to camp outside their gates, they should look to themselves. They should understand the noble national and religious traditions they inherited and understand too the ways in which those traditions had been forgotten and violated in their recent history. In their insatiable lust for wealth, the Law's strictures about justice had been overlooked; in their thirst for power, David's example of righteousness had been ignored; in their smugness, insularity and complacency, the nation's founding principles, articulated by Moses and Joshua, had been trampled under foot. If nothing else, the prophets urged, the people should at least have seen from the stories of the past what the consequences of apostasy would be.

The idea of God's constant historical presence with and provision for the people and the people's refusal to allow it to shape their lives is described by the prophet Isaiah in an allegory about a vineyard. The land has been lovingly cultivated and tended by the farmer; the vines have been planted and painstakingly nurtured. The land, however, has refused to be fertile and the vines have not grown any grapes, except bitter wild ones. The prophet imagines the farmer, God, making his case:

And now, inhabitants of Jerusalem
    and people of Judah,
judge between me and my vineyard.
What more was there to do for my vineyard
    that I have not done in it?
When I expected it to yield grapes,
    why did it yield wild grapes?
And now I will tell you
    what I will do to my vineyard.
I will remove its hedge
    and it shall be devoured.
(Isaiah 5.3–5)

Just as the prophets' denunciation of the people's behaviour is rooted in a historical awareness and perception of their life, so too is their solution to the problem. Time and time again, they challenge the people to rediscover the covenant, to look to the past and to the great heroes of the faith who show them how to live in love and faith, and to remember the faithfulness and goodness of God, in creation, vocation, salvation and daily provision. When, finally, Israel and Judah fall to their enemies and Judah is subjected to exile in Babylon, later prophets also root their descriptions of the coming restoration of the nation in the language of the rediscovery and renewal of the traditions of the past: the Law; a new line of kings in the line and of the family of David; a reflowering of justice and peace as the original, basic principles of the nation are replanted in hearts and lives. For the prophets, history is central, both to understanding the present, and to finding the key to unlock the future. Sternly and uncompromisingly, they warn us across the ages not to choose amnesia.

A similar emphasis pervades the so-called 'Wisdom' literature of the Old Testament, a collection of writings which express the deep wells of Jewish perspectives on life and faith, and reflect a body of thought that flourished about four centuries before Jesus. The Wisdom books, among them Job and Proverbs, frequently urge their readers to root their trust in God and their faith response in the witness of history. Several key events are cited frequently: creation, the escape from slavery in Egypt, the giving of the Law, and the possession of the land God promised the Israelites. God's people can place their trust in God's continued fidelity, even in times of crisis, setback and disaster, because of the reassurance of the past. They can also look to the towering figures of faith to inspire, encourage and guide them in that faith. As Job struggles with the appalling catastrophe that comes upon him, he builds the foundation of his rebuilt faith upon the ways God has blessed him in the past:

O that I were as in the months of old,
    as in the days when God watched over me;
when his lamp shone over my head. (29.2–3)

The book of Sirach, one of the so-called 'apocryphal' books not recognized by all Christians as primary scriptural material, contains a beautiful song of praise for the faith heroes of the past: kings, prophets, counsellors, leaders, poets, musicians and educators. Before describing each of them in turn, among them Moses, Elijah, David and Isaiah, the writer declares the need for and importance of such an exercise:

> Let us now sing the praises of famous men,
>> Our ancestors in their generations ...
> Their descendants stand by the covenants;
>> Their children also, for their sake.
> The assembly declares their wisdom,
>> And the congregation proclaims their praise.
> (44.1, 12, 15)

Such remembrance, with dynamic effect, allows the people of God to reflect upon their roots, on the foundation on which they build, and it also offers them a proper sense of who they are. When the writer praises God 'who fosters our growth from birth' (50.22) at the end of the hymn, he may be imagined to have meant the growth of a nation and a people enriched by faith, and not merely individuals. In recalling the family story, the people recover their identity. In all these books, Wisdom is often personified as a woman who assists and collaborates with God in everything from creation onwards. Her hand is evident nowhere more than in Israel's history, and her influence, in guiding God's people 'along a marvellous way' should never be forgotten (Wisdom 10.17).

The Psalms represent the 'worship songs' of Israel. In many respects, they are imbued with the same insights as the Wisdom tradition, and many were composed at the same time. They include frequent exhortation to the people not to forget the past and its lessons, lest they lose sight of God's faithfulness to them, or their necessary response to it. 'Our ancestors have told us, what deeds you performed in their days', exults Psalm 44, 'and we will give thanks to your name for ever' (44.1, 8). Psalms 66 and 136 celebrate the crossing of the Red Sea *en route* from slavery in Egypt to fulfilment in Canaan as the guiding memory in Israelite minds; Psalms 78 and 106 remind worshippers of the faithlessness of the people during their long journey towards freedom, and God's inexorable mercy towards them. Psalms 99 and 105 lift up heroes of faith such as Moses and Aaron. Many of the Psalms take as their starting point the life of King David, Israel's greatest king, crafting from the key events of his life heartfelt worship songs which touch the worshippers' experience as well: 23 on God's shepherdly care; 57 and 59 on danger and rescue; 51 on sin and forgiveness. Nothing is omitted, and even the disasters of the past prove helpful in remembrance and reflection: Psalm 137 recalls the exile in Babylon of the fifth century BCE, and expresses the inconsolable grief and yet dogged trust that the people felt. Psalm 126 is a jubilant memory of the return from exile and a passionate request for God to renew that experience in present difficulties:

> When the Lord restored the fortunes of Zion,
>   we were like those who dream.
> Then our mouth was filled with laughter,
>   and our tongue with shouts of joy.
>
> Restore our fortunes, O LORD ... (Psalm 126.1, 2, 4)

The ministry of Jesus of Nazareth is frequently imagined and described as one of innovation and a startling break with the past. However, though the Gospel writers do indeed present Jesus as claiming a radical new agenda, they also go out of their way to stress that Jesus himself saw his calling and purpose as rooted in and faithful to Israel's past. The birth narratives in Matthew and Luke are a case in point. They claim authority for Jesus by pointing out that he was of the line of King David and thus had the necessary pedigree to fulfil prophecy and lead Israel. In the circumstances of his birth and the events around it, key prophecies from the past were enacted and realized. As Jesus' public ministry begins, Luke describes how he goes home to Nazareth and reads from the prophet Isaiah, claiming not that it is now out of date but rather that it is fulfilled in him. Though Jesus sometimes seems to challenge

37

the Law, too, it is interesting to note that he only ever reinter-
prets it by making its demands even greater: 'You have heard
that it was said, "An eye for an eye and a tooth for a tooth."
But I say to you, Do not resist an evildoer. But if anyone strikes
you on the right cheek, turn the other also' (Matthew 5.38).
As he does so, he is careful not to claim an identity, a calling
or an understanding of God that represents any kind of break
with Israel's past. In fact, he claims to be rescuing Israel from a
misunderstanding of her past in order that she might be faithful to God in the present:

> Do not think that I have come to abolish the law or the
> prophets; I have come not to abolish but to fulfil. For truly
> I tell you, until heaven and earth pass away, not one letter,
> not one stroke of a letter, will pass from the law until all is
> accomplished.
> (Matthew 5.17–18)

Matthew and Luke record a story which dramatically makes
this claim, that Jesus represents someone in whom Israel's past
stories and identity come together in a new and yet consistent
manner. Going up a mountain with Jesus one day, some of the
disciples are privileged to see him suddenly changed – transfig-
ured – as his clothes and appearance become dazzling white.
On either side of him they see two other men, and somehow
(we are not told how) the disciples are able to recognize them
as Moses, the giver of the Law, and Elijah, the first and arguably the greatest of Israel's early prophets. This appears to be a
story about divine power, an interpretation which is apparently confirmed by the disciples hearing a voice from heaven telling them that Jesus is God's Son. Yet we need here to be clear
about what kind of power the writers mean: Jesus was never
intent on the acquisition of political power for himself, even
while he had fierce things to say to those who were. Rather,
the story is a meditation on Jesus' *authority*. Moses and Elijah
appear with Jesus in order to demonstrate Jesus' essential integ-

rity with their lives and characters; he has come to continue and even to bring to completion the work they began. Their God is Jesus' God; their calling is his calling; their purpose, calling Israel to covenant with God that the world might come to Israel's God also, is also his. Without this profoundly historical understanding of his ministry, this deep sense of his continuity with the past and faithfulness to the very tradition he was attempting to renew, Jesus would in fact have been exactly the kind of maverick preacher that his opponents wanted to make him. The startling story of the Transfiguration helps us to see this most clearly.

Jesus' faithfulness to what he sensed as his calling and mission led eventually and inevitably to conflict with the religious and secular authorities, and to a criminal's death. The earliest generation of Christians had a heavy responsibility to make sense of all this for themselves and those around them. If Jesus was the Son of God, the Messiah born of David's line who would rescue Israel and fulfil the covenant, why had he died in that way? Why, when the Law cursed anyone hanged on a tree, did Jesus meet exactly that fate? How could the claims of Jesus and the first Christians be defended? As their Jewish and pagan opponents set about the task of discrediting them, the first Christians in turn set about the task of apologetics: defending their faith and their claims. They did so, not by claiming simply that Jesus represented something new and radically different from what went before, but by relying on the kind of historical perspective which was eventually reflected in the Gospels, written a little later, and by insisting on Jesus' consistency with Israel's past. In all this, they rested their case on a claim firmly and confidently made by all those around Jesus in Jerusalem at the time of his death: that he rose from the dead. And they were led in their explanation and presentation of Jesus by one extraordinary mind: that of Paul of Tarsus.

It is impossible, of course, to encapsulate the theology of Paul in a brief paragraph or two. What is necessary here is simply to draw out his insistence that Jesus did nothing inconsistent with the faith of Israel revealed through the Law and the prophets. Paul, indeed, is the first spokesman of the view that Jesus in fact *fulfilled* the Law and the prophets in his uncompromising insistence on certain principles. Those principles, however, significantly challenged the practice of the Jewish faith as it had evolved by the time of Jesus. In other words, it was at the heart of Paul's case that Jesus was in fact calling Israel back to its true purpose and identity, as they were set out in the Hebrew Scriptures. Most important of all, Paul said, was Jesus' quite radical and, to many, shocking inclusion of non-Jews, or Gentiles, in the covenant with God. While some reacted against this as being a dangerous corruption of faith, Paul painstakingly drew out its essential coherence with the faith of Israel's past. He traced God's inclusion of the Gentiles as central to his plans and purposes back through history, and even to Abraham, the man whose response of faith and trust was the whole foundation upon which Jewish understanding was built. Even if Gentile converts to Christianity were not to be asked to follow every stricture of the Law, it was not because the Law was wrong or without value, Paul argued. It was because something better than but entirely consistent with the Law had come along in Jesus. Abraham's response of pure faith and courageous trust, long before the Law was ever given, which was entirely pleasing to God, was to act as the model also of the faith by which non-Jews could accept Jesus and be put right with God. Jesus renewed an old understanding of the Jewish faith, and represented also its fulfilment. While the consequences of his claims were outrageous to some, he did not invent something new.

Such an understanding of Paul is actually rather important, given the claims of some writers that he himself was the inventor of Christianity, taking the Jesus tradition and making out of it something quite opposed to the Judaism of his youth and quite at odds with the teachings of Jesus himself.[7] Paul was thoroughly Jewish to his fingertips, a fact of which he himself remained rather proud. He did not see himself as forsaking the faith of his forefathers in accepting the identity of Jesus as God's Messiah. His remarkable experience on the road to Damascus, which we commonly refer to as his 'conversion', ought rather to be thought of as a call, from one form of Judaism, that of his youth, to an acceptance that everything he most believed in and hoped for, as a faithful, Law-abiding Jew, was now fulfilled in Jesus. Paul's genius was to look to the past and the deep wells of his faith tradition and to draw from them resources to understand and make sense of the claims of Jesus' life, death and resurrection. He was not, like a contemporary New Age practitioner, inventing a new religion, patched together from fragments of old ones.

The New Testament concludes with some striking reflections on time and eternity, not least the Revelation to John, which describes in colourful and difficult language the way in which God in Jesus is at work within time to fulfil the purpose of creation and human life. Part of John's great vision involves the gathering in of people from every age, time and place in the great victory of Christ. Just as the book of Revelation can be seen as a response to the crisis of persecution, so too the letter to the Hebrews is a response, for Jewish Christians, to the crisis of the fall of the Jerusalem Temple in the year 70. It contains perhaps the most memorable passage in the New Testament concerning the witness of the past. In Chapter 11, the writer seeks to reassure Christians who are despairing in the face of setback and frustration. Look to the past, he says, and remember the great figures of the Jewish faith. Not one of them received in full what God promised to them, but every single one of them faithfully lived out their calling, in the trust that, through their obedience, God would be at work. They realized a vital truth: your response of faith is not just for your own good and well-being, but also for the good of those who will come after you. God's work is not confined to one generation, but is ongoing through time and eternity; your faithfulness now passes on new possibilities to the future. Indeed, he goes so far as to say that the heroes of the past *depend upon* us in the present for their faith and obedience to be fully realized and effective:

> Yet all these, though they were commended for their faith, did not receive what was promised, since God had provided something better so that they would not, without us, be made perfect. Therefore, since we are surrounded by so great a cloud of witnesses ... let us run with perseverance the race that is set before us ... (Hebrews 11.39–40; 12.1)

None of this, of course, is to say that nothing new ever happens in Christianity, or to claim that nothing genuinely fresh can ever be offered. It is not to argue for patterns of belief that never adapt or evolve over time. Those who 'do a new thing' look for resources from and consistency with the past and with the basic features of faith practised over time, but they are not imprisoned by rigid understandings which no longer apply. Jesus was claiming something startlingly original, although he saw it as profoundly rooted in and faithful to the faith practised by his ancestors for centuries. Paul knew that his ideas seemed dangerously radical to many of his fellow Jews, but asserted also that they boasted a spiritual pedigree stretching back to the first dealings of God with humanity. In this, we see a basic pattern which repeats itself time and again in the Bible, in the Church and in the life of religions generally. New situations demand new responses of faith and religious practice, and, as people of faith attempt to meet them, they discover that they need to be attentive to the understandings and responses of faithful people in the past, to the rich inheritance of faith that is theirs, as well as their present sense of the urgent need to be relevant to the modern world. They must, as the prophet advised a depressed people trying to rebuild faith and national life after a devastating setback:

> Look to the rock from which you were hewn,
> And to the quarry from which you were dug. (Isaiah 51.1)

'Updating' the Church

The Bible clearly and frequently, throughout, stresses the importance of memory in the ongoing life of faith, the need to cherish the past and apply its hard-won lessons and wisdom to current concerns. It is instructive to note that, almost every time there has been the claim of reform or renewal or change in the life of the Church, those at the centre of the change, leading the charge, have also claimed not to be inventing something new, but to be rescuing the tradition of the Church from the ways in which it has become corrupted or forgotten with the passage of time. The Church, of course, has always cherished her great thinkers and writers, the theologians who shape each succeeding generation with their unique interpretations of scripture and belief. One consequence of their work, though, can be the danger of becoming reliant on the insights of particular individuals and not remembering the wider picture of the witness of the Bible and the whole of the tradition, which often does not speak with one voice. Whenever reformers and agents of change within the Church have been effective, they have offered their agenda as the renewing of things understood in the past and now buried under the accumulation of the years. In this, their lives seem to follow the example of the biblical models and injunctions just examined: they recognize that the example of the past must be a vital ingredient in producing a response to the special challenges of the present. They looked at the 'stones', the building blocks of their faith, and answered their children's – and consciences' – questions about the meaning of it all by beginning with the foundations. What they championed, however, always seemed somehow new, for all its fidelity to the past.

The great movements of change and renewal in the medieval Church began this way, for example. Saint Francis of Assisi in the thirteenth century unleashed an extraordinary explosion of devotion and religious zeal by 'remembering' the simplicity and material poverty of Jesus and the earliest Christians. Often against the will of the Church authorities, he reminded people of the power of a simple faith, simply lived, and of the biblical and historical regard for the poor. Others reinfused the prayer and spirituality of ordinary Christians in this period by reminding them of different elements: the attraction of holiness, the beauty of creation, the benefits of discipline and obedience. In a period in which the Church seemed only to increase its wealth and power, such things often seemed particularly compelling because of their strangeness: but they all represented something foundational about the Christian faith. Richard E. Rubenstein has described how the rediscovery of the ancient Greek philosopher Aristotle, and the treatment of his work by early Christian scholars, revolutionized the life and thought of the medieval Church, and gave birth to some of the Church's finest thinkers.[8]

The greatest reformer, at the end of the medieval period, was Martin Luther. The Protestant Reformation of the sixteenth century was based on several complementary factors. Luther and his fellow reformers reminded people of the primacy of Scripture and outlined the ways in which it had been overlooked and ignored by the evolution of the Church's thinking and practice. Again, Luther's response, witnessed even more extremely in the actions of colleagues like Zwingli and then Calvin, was to urge a return to greater simplicity in public worship and private devotion: less elaborate ritual around the Mass and a different understanding of what it entailed; a reduction of the forms and objects of prayer and devotion; and a denunciation of the pope and his very worldly lifestyle. This, the Reformers claimed, was a return to pure, scriptural, 'primitive' Christianity; the Catholics replied by asserting the continuity of their faith and its practice over many centuries. A great propaganda war began, in which the authority of history and the record of the past were central.

In England, the Protestant Reformation took root in a more haphazard way than in continental Europe, shaped and often directed by the strong but competing views of the Tudor monarchs. What emerged under Elizabeth I was Anglicanism, a fascinating 'middle way' between the options for Christianity on offer overseas. The Church of England established under Elizabeth was curiously hybrid, keeping Catholic structures and clergy titles but still holding to the central tenets of Protestantism, including the sole supremacy of the Bible. For all that, though, its first founders took care to acknowledge the need for tradition itself to be renewed and updated as new occasions presented themselves. The thirty-fourth of the famous thirty-nine articles published in 1563, which defined the new church, was entitled 'on the Traditions of the Church', and stated:

> It is not necessary that Traditions and Ceremonies be in all places one, or utterly like; for at all times they have been divers, and may be changed according to the diversity of countries, times, and men's manners, so that nothing be ordained against God's Word.

The greatest theological architect of the Church of England, Richard Hooker, published a lengthy scholarly work which defended the English version of Protestantism, by using the same model. Hooker was likely the first to rest his understanding on the holding together of Scripture and tradition, on the need to be faithful to the Bible while still attentive to the ways in which the faith, and the Church, had evolved over time. He claimed authority and authenticity for the English Church, as representing an unbroken line of succession with the Christians of the past, while alert and responsive to a vastly changed environment.

Nearly two centuries later, John Wesley took this basis seriously, in challenging the Church of England to return to its roots, remember its Lord and recover its original identity. Methodism too was born because of a predilection for the past, and a desire to see old ways brought to life for a present need. Many of Wesley's characteristic emphases, both theological and practical, were born from his own rediscovery of

Scripture and tradition: open-air preaching, an insistence on the possibility of human perfection through divine inspiration, a clear bias to the poor, a passionate belief in the universality of God's grace. Wesley published a multi-volume collection, *The Christian Library*, in which he sought to make available to ordinary Christians the treasures of the great Christians of the past and thus foster their spiritual life and understanding; many of the authors he chose were from the earliest centuries of the Church. Methodism was, he always claimed, a plea for a return to 'primitive' Christianity: the pure faith once lived by the first followers of Jesus. And, just as Methodism grew from a love for the Church of England and a desire to see its renewal, so in time William Booth's 'Salvation Army' arose from his perception that Methodism in turn had lost touch with its roots and needed to recover its memory in order to fulfil its high calling, especially by serving the poor in Christ's name.

Forty years after Wesley, a group of scholarly Anglicans argued for the Church of England to renew its understanding of its debt to Roman Catholicism and to reconnect itself to the historical Church in theology, worship and prayer. The 'Oxford Movement', as their group became known, has been described as all about seeking the renewal of tradition. John Henry Newman, John Keble, Edward Pusey and their associates felt that the evolution of its Protestant identity had taken the church too far from its Catholic roots, and severed it too much from its heritage. Though to some their effort looked impossibly backward, an attempt to undo four centuries of history, it brought a good deal of freshness and energy to the English Church, in liturgy, preaching, pastoral care and a new concern for 'the beauty of holiness'. That reinvigoration is still evident and felt today, and contributes greatly to the breadth of the Anglican Church, as well as to its life of worship, service and prayer.

Such a survey of some of the most obvious renewal movements within the Church makes the point: new energy is released when Christians rediscover their past and cultivate their memories. This is consistent too with the witness of Scripture. Other groups and parties within the Church have broken away because of their recovery of different elements from the past and voices within the tradition. We shall think about this more deeply in examining the current ecumenical context later on, but will end with a recent example of modernization in the largest portion of the Church. Modern Catholics are inescapably shaped by the events of the late 1950s and 1960s. The elderly Pope John XXIII surprised the world in 1958 by summoning a council of all the church's bishops – the so-called Second Vatican Council – at which he and his advisers pushed beyond the innate intransigence of the church's hierarchy and brought forth profound change in the church's teaching. Pope John, who died before it could be completed, said that the council was an exercise in *aggiornamento*: 'updating' the Church. Among other things, the council spoke for the first time about the wickedness perpetrated by the Church to those of other faiths, especially the Jews, and set the scene for further efforts to re-engage with the modern world and seek reconciliation with those estranged from religious life. In all of this though, the 'updating' was never described as something wholly new. The architects of the council, rather, understood that they were reaching deeper into the tradition, deeper into the voices of the past, to recover spiritual treasures, of compassion, justice and love, which human bigotry and hatred had rejected in the name of religion. In doing so, they were following in a long line of reformers, and were being attentive to the injunctions of scripture and the example of the saints: as well as the needs of a changing world.

Mention of 'the saints' reminds us that Christians are members of a big family. It spans the globe, and stretches back through time, 2,000 years back to the birth of Jesus, but thousands of years further back too, through our Jewish ancestors. In life together, in prayer and worship and service, in finding the courage to speak out and the perseverance to see things through, Christians believe in the power of remembering those who have gone before. They believe in it, because of the lessons they can learn, and the ways in which they can receive profound insights from the past. They also believe in what they call the 'Communion of Saints': that such remembering is not merely an act of memory but also one of real presence. As Buechner says, in some sense it summons those who have died back into our consciousness and company, and allows them to shape our outlook and our responses. It gives us the resources we need to be faithful to the challenge of faith in our time and place, as they were in theirs. It enables us radically to challenge and change the status quo on occasion, and in so doing still be absolutely faithful to what has gone before. God, who ultimately remembers and cherishes us all, holds us together in community, as family, for all time.

My grandma taught me many things: the value of humour, a love of singing and hymnody, the importance of family affection and loyalty. Those things live on in me. At certain times, they are vividly present to me: and so is she, though long dead. In my life of faith too, I need places, like a family Christmas, in which I can allow the voices and shaping influences of the past to become more real and tangible, clearer and stronger, as I forge my own spiritual life and make my own choices about the future. All Christians need this. In worship, in prayer, in study and meditation, those voices, those saints, are present, because held in the eternal life of God. To refuse to listen to them, to be a deliberate amnesiac, is to choose childishness, aimlessness and impotence. The American poet and farmer Wendell Berry puts it beautifully, reflecting on the responsibility of those gathered around a graveside in his native Kentucky:

> What we owe the future
> is not a new start, for we can only begin
> with what has happened. We owe the future
> the past, the long knowledge
> that is the potency of time to come.
> That makes of a man's grave a rich furrow.

The community of knowing in common is the seed
of our life in this place. There is not only
no better possibility, there is no
other, except for chaos and darkness,
the terrible ground of the only possible
new start. And so as the old die and the young
depart, where shall a man go who keeps
the memories of the dead, except home
again, as one would go back after a burial,
faithful to the fields, lest the dead die
a second and more final death.[9]

Notes

1 Frederick Buechner, *Whistling in the Dark*, quoted in Buechner, *Listening to Your Life*, comp. G. Connor, San Francisco: Harper San Francisco, 1992, p. 14.

2 Quoted in F. H. Thompsett, *Living with History*, Cambridge: Cowley, 1999, p. 167.

3 He was actually quoting the Hindu scripture, the Bhagavad-Gita, 11.32.

4 Quoted in a letter to Robert Hooke, 5 February 1676.

5 *The Tempest*, Act 2, Scene 1, ll. 243–4.

6 Rowan Williams, *Why Study the Past?: The Quest for the Historical Church*, London: Darton, Longman and Todd, 2005, p. 29.

7 For example, A. N. Wilson, *Paul: The Mind of the Apostle*, New York: W. W. Norton, 1998.

8 Richard E. Rubenstein, *Aristotle's Children: How Christians, Muslims and Jews Rediscovered Ancient Wisdom and Illuminated the Middle Ages*, Orlando: Harcourt, 2003.

9 Wendell Berry, 'At a Country Funeral', from *The Selected Poems of Wendell Berry*, New York: Counterpoint, 1998, p. 92.

3

RE-CALCULATING WHAT
HAS GONE

Interpreting Christian History

History – good history – is far more than a chronicle of what happened when. History written that way is indeed what Winston Churchill once jokingly called it: 'one damn thing after another', and doesn't really help us very much. The craft of history involves a whole range of skills and gifts, and historians sometimes even have a debate with and among themselves about what exactly it entails. Historians cannot recreate the conditions and events of the past, nor exactly reproduce them, like scientists in the laboratory, and they can never claim to have paid attention to every single participant in any given event. Nor can they ever make more than provisional conclusions, open to the correction and critique of others' research or their own. They need to be open to a range of events, as much of the background as possible, and to multiple voices within the historical narrative. They also need imagination to make the past (which is, after all, a 'foreign country' in which things were done differently)[1] come alive, judgement to sift between differing viewpoints, and courage to come up with conclusions at the end of it all.

Historians have sometimes had difficulty with the judgement part. That will be something that particularly concerns Christians, attempting to discern from their faith history what is of importance and use in the present. The extent to which we are called to make moral judgements on the actions and motivations of people from the past will be something we shall have to consider later. It is enough for now to note that it is a subject which has generated debate between historians, and which illustrates the need to avoid two errors in considering the past: treating it as exactly like the present except in fancy dress, and treating it as something so unlike our own time that is has nothing to say.[2] E. H. Carr, in his masterly study *What Is History?*, published in 1961, put it succinctly: 'interpretation', he claimed, 'is the life-blood of history'.[3]

So then, what might this process of discovery and interpretation look like or resemble? It is worth considering what historians, even amateur ones, are doing, and how they work, when they attempt to make the past speak to the present and shape the future in the ways we have been considering. Sometimes, history has been thought of as a science, although it clearly belongs among the 'humanities' in school faculties and departments. By this, we mean that history requires disciplines and methods, like any other pursuit of knowledge, and identifying what those methods are, and the process by which we go about them, helps us better to understand what it is we are doing. As we have already seen, history is not like chemistry, in which experiments can be repeated many times to prove the same thing; the conditions and events of the past can never be summoned into the present exactly as they were, in all their detail and enormity, in order to draw firm conclusions from them. So, what kind of 'science' is history?

The American military historian, John Lewis Gaddis, makes a number of helpful analogies in his book, *The Landscape of History*, written partly as a response to Carr's classic work. His insights may help us understand how interpretations of our Christian past 'work'. Gaddis offers the science of palaeontology, the study of fossils, as an example of the historian's art as well. Palaeontologists, using their scientific equipment and understanding, look at relics of a very far distant past, and deduce from those remains the realities which produced them. He calls this the derivation of 'past processes from present structures', and explains:

> The same thing happens every day in natural history museums before critical audiences of small children. What's the reconstruction of dinosaurs and other ancient creatures from fossils, after all, if not a fitting of imagined flesh to surviving bones, or at least to impressions of them? And the kids are, most of the time at least, suitably impressed.[4]

Historians do a very similar thing, though they start not with fossils, but with artifacts, memories, written accounts or simply the way things are as we inherit them.

Gaddis offers two other striking images for the historical method. One is that of the cartographer, or map-maker. People who draw maps are obviously unable exactly to reproduce the thing they are charting: a landscape. Rather, they have to create something which accurately represents that landscape, at a much smaller scale. The result helps people in a variety of ways, in detailing contours that they cannot foresee and suggesting routes between places which they may not know. Like map-makers, historians must make judgements about the available information and make choices about what to include and what to omit. They have to distil the experiences and observations of others to help us navigate our way forward. Secondly, and more quirkily, Gaddis uses the image of tailors: who 'represent' the bodies of their clients to the world. Like historians, tailors start with what is there, interpret this reality through different viewpoints using their imagination and conscious of contemporary tastes and trends, and finally place the result before an audience. And here comes the critical piece, for all the varied disciplines to which Gaddis is referring:

> The patrons may approve because what they see confirms their preconceptions. They may disapprove if it does not. Or

– and this is what paleontologists, tailors and cartographers as well as historians hope for – the product may move those who encounter it to revise their own views so that a new basis for critical judgement emerges, perhaps even a new view of reality itself.[5]

This may all seem a little too remote and out of reach. But we are all engaged at some level in making these judgements about history. To take one recent example, 30 March 2002 was a significant moment. It marked the death of Her Majesty Queen Elizabeth the Queen Mother, whose life of royal service had spanned two centuries, and who became a figure held in deep affection by millions, not just in Britain. The Queen Mother represented something quite special, particularly in the minds of the British: tenacity, perseverance and sheer longevity, and something also of the British spirit, through her resilience and encouragement of many through the Second World War. When she died, at the great age of 101, many felt the passing of a whole era, and even a turning point of history. A woman born in the reign of Queen Victoria, just eight months into the twentieth century, died in an age vastly different from and scarcely conceivable by that into which she arrived. Along the course of her life, too, she seemed to have been not merely subject to the course of history, but one who shaped it. As the obituary writers set about summarizing how she changed British identity and culture, and what her unprecedented contribution would mean in the ongoing life of the nation, the Poet Laureate, Andrew Motion, wrote these lines about her burial site in Windsor:

Think of the buried body laid
inside its final earthly shade,

in darkness like a solid cloud
where weight and nothing coincide,

in silence which will never break
unless real angels really speak,

while we who wait our turn live on
re-calculating what has gone –

time-tested dignity and pride
and finished work personified.[6]

It is this task, of 're-calculating what has gone', which occupies
historians. But it's also a task in which every one who takes an
interest in events is involved. When, on the Queen Mother's
death, we asked ourselves, 'What difference did she make?',
we were doing just that. When we concluded that her influence
on events and her shaping of current British reality was for the
good, we were doing just that. We looked at her life, the world
she inherited and the world she left behind, and made judgements about the connection between the two. And, if we take
seriously the call to remember the past, something rather similar is the task of Christians. The most difficult thing, though,
is to know what the past is really saying to us, what tradition's
wisdom is for our age and time. Faced with the sheer weight of
our history, its multiple voices and events and the appearance
of constant change and evolution in Christian thought, how
are we ever to 'mine the meaning' of Christian history today?
If our history is a living, breathing tradition which speaks to
and informs our faith response in the here and now, how do
we begin to understand and assimilate it? Let us then examine
that task, and consider how to 're-calculate what has gone' in
ways that give us life and renew our faith.

The hermeneutics of history

If exploring the record of our faith history in order to discover
its wisdom for today seems like a tough, and rather subjective,
enterprise, we would do well to remember that something very
similar is going on in our churches every single Sunday morning. When preachers get into the pulpit and begin to offer a
message, they are acting as historians. By that I mean that they

are taking a text from an ancient, distant culture and time and attempting to interpret it for the present, to offer from it something which speaks to a faith community in vastly different circumstances than those for whom it was first written. Think of the Bible as a fossil for a moment: the preacher is trying to put flesh on it. Or, again, think of the preacher as a map-maker, outlining the contours of the strange territory of biblical times, and navigating a course through it that moves the whole listening congregation along on their faith journey. As with Gaddis's various professions too, the preacher is equally subject to finding that their conclusions do not sit too well with their hearers' own sense of what they should be being told!

Although it is at one level a historical document like any other, the Bible also forms the principal authority for Christian life and faith, and thus we privilege it with a place all of its own in study, learning and theological college syllabuses. Particular attention – which sadly they often forget all too soon after leaving college – is given to training clergy in the art of biblical interpretation. It is especially vital for people who will preach and lead God's people for their whole lives that they understand how to do this: how to understand a passage in its own context before making the leap to their own; how to recognize a faithful interpretation from a distortion or from fundamentalism; how to avoid the easy pitfalls of misleading their hearers into false conclusions. The name which we give to this whole process, the process of making the Bible speak from an ancient culture into the present day, is 'hermeneutics'. It comes from a Greek root, meaning simply, 'interpretation'. Hermeneutics most commonly refers to the interpretation of the Bible, but the disciplines and methods of hermeneutics should also inform what we are doing when we study the past, especially our Christian past. As we begin to see how faithfully to undertake a study of our Christian history, we should keep good biblical hermeneutics in mind.

Some preachers, of course, claim that when they preach they are not involved in a hermeneutical exercise. They are not, they say, interpreting anything, but rather allowing the Bible to speak for itself. The best advice for them, in the words of the great American preacher Fred Craddock, is that 'they need to get over this'. Preaching, if it isn't dangerous, unfiltered fundamentalism, is always interpretative. However direct and clear the parallel seems to be between an ancient text and a modern situation, there is always an exercise in cross-cultural translation going on. It is irresponsible not to bear that in mind. The point is that we do not think it is an impossible task; indeed, Christians above all people perhaps have most reason to believe in such historical interpretation and its value and purpose: they seek to offer some form of it from their pulpits and in their small groups and classes every week, and for the benefit not just of an edu-cated elite but of people of all backgrounds, ages and kinds.

We saw in Chapter 1 how this interpretative process can fre-quently be necessary in making laws and governing countries. In that context, as in a Christian one, it is a process about making value judgements, and the forming of character and identity. So, as we study the events, peoples and currents of the Christian past, how do we make them make sense for today? What – and how – do they teach us? How can we know that our 'reading' of our tradition is correct? And, most of all, by what process do we assimilate the stories of our past and allow them to inform our present and future? Before we consider spe-cific themes and currents in Christian history and their witness to us today, let us think about ten questions by which we might engage in historical enquiry. They are ten questions central to any hermeneutical method, and therefore questions which should be as familiar to a preacher as they are to historians. In dealing with any story from the past, these are some of the questions we need to bear in mind.

Question 1: Who are the authors or participants in this story?

This is the obvious place to begin. It makes the world of differ-ence, naturally, to know, when hearing a story about Martin

Luther, that he was a sixteenth-century German monk who was led by his conscience and experience to ask some serious questions about his own Roman Catholic Church. In time, these questions led to the Protestant Reformation. At the same time, Ulrich Zwingli in Switzerland was pursuing a similar agenda, but from a very different background, which vitally affected his own approach. Whereas Luther emerged from the monastic cloisters, Zwingli had been a political insider and military chaplain, and was eventually to die in battle, and not, like Luther, in his bed. Zwingli brought to his reforming of Zurich a self-confidence and composure that the insecure and psychologically troubled Luther sought all his life. Zwingli, too, took the programme they basically shared much further, unhindered by Luther's desire to cling to some of the old customs and forms of worship which he loved. To take another Reformation example, in reading a narrative from the past it is vital to know who was writing, and from what perspective, broadly speaking. The English martyrologist John Foxe wrote a history of the Church to defend the integrity of Protestantism and highlight what he saw as Catholic cruelty. If we were to read Foxe's account, we would need to understand something about the axe he was grinding and the perspective from which he wrote. In fact, a failure adequately to do this work led to Catholicism being viewed as a cruel and vengeful religion for many years: the victors in the Reformation struggles in England were shaped for generations by their own authors.

As we begin the process of forming thumbnail sketches of the players in our stories, it is also important to place them against the background of the whole of their life. No great figure of history emerged from the womb believing everything they would ever believe. For all of us, both humble and great, the changes in our outlook, view, belief and conviction as we mature are vital parts of our story. St Francis of Assisi was born into great wealth and the expectation of worldly power and influence. His rejection of those things, and the process by which it came about, profoundly affected his character and the practice of Christianity he advocated. They are an integral part of his story, and shape its themes. They also influence our interpretation of it. So with Ignatius of Loyola, another young nobleman and soldier of the sixteenth century, who came to a newer depth of faith through a long period spent convalescing from battle wounds. The Spiritual Exercises which Ignatius later wrote for the members of his new religious order, the Jesuits, are the direct result of that period of depression, enforced inactivity and subsequent conversion. So too was his insistence on a life of poverty, service and disciplined charity. Finally, the life of the nineteenth-century cardinal John Henry Newman, whom we shall meet in a later chapter, bears very careful study for this kind of movement and change. Interpreters of it need to be attentive to the slow evolution of his views, leading up to his decision to leave the Church of England and convert to Roman Catholicism.

Question 2: For what audience was this written? To whom is the message directed?

This is a question often more relevant to historical accounts than to the actions of individuals, though not exclusively. Just as it makes all the difference in the world to know that Luke's Gospel was written for a primarily Gentile readership, or that many of Isaiah's prophecies are aimed at the influential elite in Jerusalem, so too we should understand something of the people for whom figures from the past were writing or to whom they were making their appeal. John Wesley's sermons are standard fare for preacher training and ministerial formation: but there is quite a revealing difference between those delivered to the educated congregations of Oxford and those declaimed in the open air in England's industrial heartlands. Knowing something about the nature and character of the addressees of Dietrich Bonhoeffer's prison letters, or of Martin Luther King's *Letter from Birmingham Jail*, similarly, shapes the way in which those documents must be read. Just as preachers 'tailor' (to use an earlier metaphor) their sermons for particular congregations, so too do historical writers of all types and of all times.

Perhaps this question is faced most acutely when we study the written records of the early Church. In this context especially, the issue of genre – the form and purpose of something – is very important. When we say the Creed in church, we are using a statement created and shaped by Christians in solemn assembly 2,000 years ago whose fundamental assertions about God we still cherish. The leaders of the Church in those days crafted it for commendation to all the faithful; and the leaders of the Church today continue to do the same. We thus share with those far distant ancestors both the responsibility to receive it humbly and the need to interpret it in our life, our community and our world. Quite the same level of authority does not attach to other kinds of documents, because they are more specific and addressed to definite contexts. That is not to say, though, that they say nothing to us. Antony the Hermit's advice to those seeking to live a desert life of prayerful withdrawal, Irenaeus of Lyons' rebuttal of the heresy of Marcion, or Eusebius' stirring and fortifying account of the deaths of the martyrs were addressed to sets of people and circumstances utterly dissimilar from us and ours. These writings still challenge us to attempt to summon to mind through an act of imagination their first readers and hearers, with all their struggles, hopes and needs. By doing this, we begin to try to appreciate the impact these writings had then, before we make an attempt to make them speak faithfully to our lives.

Question 3: What is the context?

This is perhaps the most important initial question of all, and the one which in biblical study tends to be the most neglected. By it, we mean what is the background to this piece, or this life, or this event? To what is it responding and by what is it shaped? Biblical scholars use a German phrase which helps us to understand what this stage involves; they talk about a passage's *Sitz im Leben*, or 'situation in life'. It is the question which can involve the most work and detailed effort. By context, we mean a range of issues and questions: the country in which something occurs or is created; the period, of course, against which it happens; the immediate surroundings, whether urban or rural, the farm or the university, the home, monastery or corridors of power. We also must have at least in the back of our minds a sense of what happened after or because of the event or piece we are studying. Let us return to Martin Luther for an example. In 1517, he nailed 95 'theses', or statements, to the door of the castle church in Wittenburg. The theses were a stinging critique of Roman Catholic life and practice, and demanded significant renewal. It is generally agreed that this event was a primary catalyst in the birth of the Protestant Reformation, whose consequences were to be so great for all subsequent Christian life and thought. Now, to appreciate the force and impact of Luther's action, we would need to understand something about its context, in several ways: the late medieval Church and its life, especially in Luther's Germany; the rise of new methods of learning and new approaches to thought which had deeply influenced European intellectual life; Luther's own development as a human being and as a Christian theologian at home, monastery and university; and the response which his theses quickly provoked in the hearts and lives of many people. Only with at least a little knowledge of each does the event make any sense.

The same exercise is important for more recent times too. The First Amendment to the US Constitution, guaranteeing freedom of religion, was a response to the religion of the British colonies of the seventeenth and eighteenth centuries, which had often been repressive, intolerant and even violent. It showed clear intellectual debts to the pacifism of the 'Enlightenment' movement, and theologically reflected its Deist faith, but also the inclusiveness of the Quakers. It continues to excite debate in contemporary American politics and religion. These are the kinds of contexts which we must consider. Finally, the life of Pope John Paul II is impossible to assess without some knowledge of Communist Eastern Europe, his own formation in Poland and rise through the Catholic hierarchy, and the Liberation Theologies of South America. His career makes its particular contribution to Christian history because of the popes whom he succeeded and the way in which he represented something of a retreat from the progressive air of the Second Vatican Council. To skip this kind of investigative phase of our thinking leaves us open to terrible misunderstanding, in which we could variously decide to advocate the burning of heretics in town centres, or, as John Wesley was known to do, forbid the drinking of tea. Modern Methodists not least would find both ideas repugnant. Where preachers at this point turn to their commentaries, Christians discovering their past need a library of helpful resources to help them too. They do not need to be experts; but they do need to be curious and committed enough to do a little spade work.

Question 4: What, in the original context, was being said or done?

Having placed the author or protagonist in their context, against their background, we are nearer to being able to understand what their life, or writing, meant *in its original context*. We do not fully understand, for example, the extraordinary pioneering work of St Clare of Assisi in the thirteenth century unless we have taken on board something of the papacy in that period and the institutional resistance of the Church hierarchy to new forms of women's ministry. Against that canvas, her achievements seem all the more powerful and unlikely. A complex and lengthy treatise like St Augustine's *City of God* might offer insights at a face-value reading, for those with the patience to persevere with it. It makes infinitely more sense to a twenty-first-century mind, however, when we set it properly against the backdrop of the fall of the Roman Empire to the Goths in 410 and Augustine's deepening anxiety about what he saw as the collapse of Christian civilization. From that quite turbulent and disturbing period of history, his theological reflection takes its foundation and major themes, consoling his readers by affirming that only by divine help can humanity reach its potential, never purely through political control.

This may sound a daunting process: but, in reality, we are more familiar with the way it works than we might suppose, more used to this process of having to make deductions about writings from another time and culture than we imagine. The BBC's adaptations of Geoffrey Chaucer's *Canterbury Tales* were watched by a huge audience. The modern setting of the television plays, and the stories they told, however, depended upon a prior investigation, of removing from the tales what was unfamiliar and dissimilar because of the distance of time, and extracting the essential message which Chaucer was communicating to his own readers and time. This message was subsequently reclothed in a contemporary story, setting and language: but the essence was the same, stories of lust, greed, love, honour and virtue. Another example of television fame concerns the incomparable novels of Jane Austen. While we may not share the attitudes of the eighteenth century about teenage sexual behaviour, we understand when reading (or watching) *Pride and Prejudice* why Lydia's elopement with Mr Wickham was so disastrous for the Bennett family. And we understand, too, the basic and 'universally acknowledged truth' that Austen was making about folly, selfishness and family honour. It is a point that we appreciate in the present too: but that is to jump ahead in the hermeneutical process.

Question 5: How did others respond to this, at the time?

Just as important as what someone did, said or wrote is the reaction that they provoked in those around them. To use two earlier examples: St Clare fostered a great rise in women's religious life as many caught her vision and decided to follow her example. As a consequence, the Poor Clares grew into a significant monastic movement. Martin Luther found that he had tapped into widespread feelings about the Church and articulated a number of concerns which found a receptive audience. The ripple effect of his actions was dramatic, and resulted in schism and a number of new Christian groups. In his case especially, it is significant to note the ways in which others took his insights in new and quite different directions, building on his work while making it their own. John Calvin's religious regime in Geneva, for example, was quite impossible without Luther's work, and drew significantly from his thought, but Calvin lived and worked a generation after Luther, and elaborated his theology in some quite distinctive ways. Also to be noted here would be the kinds of opposition or critique to which people were subjected at the time of their life or writing. Responding from the mindset of their day, critics often illustrate more clearly what was at stake and what was being said at the time. Some ancient Christian writings are known to us only because books written against them survive though they do not; it is thus possible to piece them together from their opponent's work. More commonly, critical reaction simply reveals a movement, figure or event more fully, as with the reaction to the early Methodist movement from both the Anglican establishment and the intellectual elite, or the unrelenting mockery of William Booth's 'Salvation Army' from the governing classes, which demonstrated clearly its character as a movement of the poor and working classes. Supremely, contemporary reaction both positive and negative to a past event tells us a great deal about what was significant about it. We shall turn to this in more depth in a moment.

Question 6: What voices am I not hearing? Which are excluded?

This is a much more difficult question to answer – but it's important to try. One of the reasons why Christian history in particular has been subjected to such criticism is that it contains so much which, in a twenty-first-century context, seems to condemn it. One of the main arguments of this book is that, in rediscovering something of the depth and breadth of our history, in unearthing the 'hidden' voices within it, we shall in the process rediscover its riches. History is usually written by those in power, those who have 'won'. That is why it can be so difficult to hear the voices of women, for instance, in studying the past. But it is essential, either to dig deeper until we find those voices, or to be conscious of their silence, and to try and ask imaginative questions to help reconstruct them. It is also quite difficult sometimes to hear the voices of ordinary Christians: the 'men and women in the pew', if you will. They have not tended to be the ones recording their thoughts and experiences for posterity. It is possible, however, to find some indications of their experience or, at the very least, to try and recreate it. To offer one example: the so-called 'Puritan' movement of the Elizabethan Church in late sixteenth-century England felt that the reforms within the Church of England had not gone far enough in 'cleaning up' the faults and failures of the Roman Catholic past. They demanded greater simplicity and deeper piety and even formed a whole sub-culture around their convictions, while also calling on the government for action. If we read the accounts of this that come from the Church hierarchy, we see the Puritan movement, often, as a rebellious, subversive, holier-than-thou thorn in its side. If, however, we turn to some of the surviving personal accounts written by Puritans about their life and religion, a rather touching and moving picture emerges of a simple effort to take Scripture seriously and cultivate a life of prayer and integrity. A similar gulf, to which historians must pay close attention, exists between grassroots accounts of the Catholic 'ecclesial communities' in Central and South America in the 1960s that birthed the radical 'Liberation Theology' movements and the Vatican documents that condemned them, troubled by what they saw as tendencies towards Communism. It is vital, either to discover as many voices as possible, or imaginatively to try and locate them.

Question 7: Does this show continuity with what went before? Or something strikingly new?

This, of course, is a basic and essential historical question. The writings of the New Testament emerge because something quite new within the life and faith of Judaism was thought to have arrived in the person of Jesus. As we have seen, this was precisely the question Paul was trying to address and work through in his letters, outlining for the earliest Christians what Jesus meant and what faith in him would challenge and change. This kind of development of traditional ways of thinking and believing is always interesting and significant to notice, whether it is revealed in apparently sudden and dramatic ways (the Protestant Reformation) or more subtle ones (the gradual opening up of Church leadership to women over several centuries). It is often in finding such moments of change that we also discover something of the disturbing and quite radical power of the Christian tradition, and its ability occasionally to be quite bold in rejecting the surrounding culture and 'doing a new thing'. Rowan Williams puts it well:

> When we examine a past period, we should ... ask what it was that made it impossible for Christians simply to repeat what had been said; we should look for what was not simply the reflection of cultural attitudes ... if [we] are looking for signs of the act of God in the Church, [we] will be looking in each period for what unsettles the Church, what appears with increasing urgency as unfinished business.[7]

One striking illustration of this, which Williams talks about and which we shall examine in greater depth later on, is the way in which Christian attitudes towards slavery changed over the years. Having generally (though not universally) accepted the surrounding belief, reflected in the New Testament, that slavery was an acceptable human institution, Christians by the eighteenth century were beginning to change their minds.

Eventually, of course, men like John Wesley and William Wilberforce launched a great and costly campaign to abolish the slave trade and end the evils of slave ownership for good. This was a moment of change, of *discontinuity* with the past to which it is necessary to pay close attention. Being attentive to moments or movements of change also helps us to understand how tradition itself is a fluid thing which can adapt to new situations and demands, and not a straitjacket, unchanging over time and across distance.

Question 8: How does this story show the rediscovery of things forgotten?

This clearly follows from the previous question and reminds us again to search for those more muted voices. People and events easily become hidden and obscured by some of the processes we have mentioned: white male control, being on the losing side, or having the wrong kind of background. We should never allow our assumptions about our tradition to blind us to its ongoing ability to challenge and change us, along the lines which Gaddis was earlier quoted as describing. The tradition sometimes speaks *against* itself in contrary voices, and appreciating and working through that will be a key feature of this interpretative process as well. Those who interpret the historical record for their communities have always to be the kind of people who never lose their ability to be surprised, and to be open to unexpected discoveries which call them to unimagined conclusions. To offer one concrete example, we might think of Archbishop Oscar Romero, appointed to the highest office in the El Salvadorean Church in 1977 at a time of great disruption, deep poverty and manifold breaches of human rights in that country. Romero, to the disappointment of many, came to such power with a track record of conservatism and a refusal to criticize the country's leadership, in accordance with the Vatican's instructions to priests in the region. Experience, however, and the renewal in his soul of the long Christian tradition of justice, peace and the rights of the poor led him instead, and against the Pope's will, to a position of prominence and passionate prophetic engagement with the corrupt authorities of his country. In time, that bias to the poor led to his assassination at the altar. His reading of the Church's tradition led him to such an interpretative leap: and to risk his own life in the cause of truth, peace and integrity.

Question 9: How do I hear the story? What in me does it speak to?

In any interpretative process, whether with the Bible, a historical process or a current event, it is vital to be as self-aware as possible, to understand our own perspective, and to realize the angle from which we approach the task. Even when we think we are being even-handed and open to realities quite different from our own, we still need to do the hard work of trying to be aware of how something speaks to us in different ways, reinforcing worldviews we already possess, challenging us to new ones, or opening us up to those which we have never encountered before. The kinds of personal identities we are talking about here fall into several different categories. Gender and sexuality, of course, matter greatly, given that so much Christian history, like so much biblical material, is acted out and recorded by white, heterosexual men. Our denominational background matters also: it will always be difficult but essential to be willing to envision our own denomination in new ways, and to overcome instinctive prejudices against others as we learn more of their character and development over time. Another key element will be ethnicity; to use the example of slavery, the way in which we read the accounts of the abolition of the slave trade may be considerably affected by which side of that racial divide we are on. The story of the Church's involvement with and ministry alongside the poor assumes different proportions too depending on our socio-economic background; our understanding of its interactions with surrounding societies and prevailing cultures is somewhat conditioned by our own political philosophy and commitments. David Holgate and Rachel Starr, writing about biblical interpretation, recommend the regular practice of 'defining' ourselves before embarking upon any reading of a text.[8] Here again, the same is true of any historical reading. Making a shift between historical settings is no easy exercise, and those who claim that it is are often perpetrators of all manner of fundamentalism, and even wickedness. The scant involvement of women in leadership through much of the Church's life might appeal to the desire of chauvinistic misogynists to marginalize them in the present; but such a reading would have paid no attention to the 'context' of such views in the present, so greatly at odds with the prevailing collective wisdom. Before using the historical record glibly to bolster my views, I need to be self-aware enough to identify those views, and to recognize that not everyone shares them, and that not everyone will read the historical record from my perspective – quite the reverse. The ways in and extent to which something attracts, repels or challenges me are defined by these basic questions of identity. Given the fundamental importance of this kind of self-discipline in historical (and biblical) interpretation, one could actually make the case that it is very good for the soul!

Question 10: How, finally, do I 're-calculate the past' here? What does it mean, in my life and in this context?

Once we have contextualized both the story or events we are dealing with, and attempted to identify also our own responses to them and from where in us and our situation they arise, we are at the threshold of the imaginative leap of interpretation. The word 'imaginative' is apt because, as we shall see, there will never be only one interpretation of anything: back to the point just made about fundamentalism. And the answers may not be obvious! The process here becomes creative, like poetry or music: anyone who has tried to write poetry knows that it involves hard work. Perhaps an experience or thought will trigger an idea or image, but poets have to work to hone and refine their thoughts so that the end result accurately reflects what they wanted to present. They also know about the need to make the leap of imagination between one reality and another, between an initial impetus to write and the representation of that experience on paper and in words. What images will they use? How will they reflect upon experience? Composers undergo this too, translating a place, experience or feeling into different modes of expression and deciding what notes, framework and musical forces they will use. Mendelssohn's *Hebrides* overture vividly depicts a swirling Scottish sea and the majesty of the cliffs; Tchaikovsky's Sixth Symphony is a powerful, almost devastating expression of personal grief; Richard Strauss's song *Im Abendrot* is perhaps the most beautiful reflection on old age and death ever conceived. All of these illustrate this process at work. Something very similar is going on in preaching, too. When preachers use the story of Jacob at Peniel to talk about their own struggles with faith, or Jesus calming the storm to reflect on a turbulent period in their own life or that of the world, they are translating one event into another context, and interpreting an insight from the biblical setting to the modern one by a great, imaginative, poetic leap of faith. Historical interpreters need to be poets and artists!

What is tantalizing and energizing about this is that it is impossible to be more detailed about the end result of the interpretative process. Whereas the previous questions have usually had rather definite answers, this is the final creative stage, at which, if the necessary work has been done, anything is possible, new insights are born and fresh energy is generated. This is both the excitement of the hermeneutical process and, for many, also its fear. As E. H. Carr said, 'good historians ... whether they think about it or not, have the future in their bones. Besides the question Why? the historian also asks the question Whither?'[9] And, as everybody knows, mapping out the next stages of our journey, deciding what is next for us, personally or collectively, can be a daunting and even frightening experience, even as it entices us. This is an open-ended process which, as we have seen, has the capacity to shock and transform us. That is because, if attempted carefully, prayerfully and attentively, it is a process driven by the unpredictable Spirit of God. Holgate and Starr quote Brian Blount:

> Since we're always changing, and our contexts are always changing, the words that interpret the whisper of God's Spirit in our time must necessarily be changing as well. God, you remember Jesus saying, is a God of the living, not of the dead. But a last word is necessarily a dead word. It stops listening. It stops learning. It stops living![10]

'A past that promised more': applying our interpretations

Brutal, dictatorial regimes have a record of doing a twisted version of this kind of interpretation of the past for their citizens: they manipulate history in order for everyone to have the same understanding of the reasons why the current government is and was necessary. They alter the facts and skew their transmission so as to quell dissent and create an unchallengeable myth about the country. Stalin's Soviet Union was a classic example of this trend. Those who offered alternative versions of the past were summarily dismissed to labour camps far away. It's worth bearing this in mind, simply to reiterate the point that Christian history cannot work this way, however much we are tempted to nail our understanding of ourselves down and bar any other interpretations. Even scientists like palaeontologists have to acknowledge that, however careful their data collection and however expert their analysis of it, there is always room for varied interpretations of the evidence and for discoveries of entirely new fossilized remains that might alter the picture. Map-makers have to update their work as new roads are built and as the landscape changes, whether through building, erosion, volcanic activity or climate change. Christians, living in a changing world and constantly making new discoveries about their past, must always be humble enough to know that their interpretations are provisional. Indeed, in that lies something of the nature of faith itself, which is not faith if it claims to have every belief and every piece of understanding locked down.

During the Reformation period, some of the greatest literary struggles were around competing claims for continuity and authenticity in the Church's past, the Catholics pointing to the unbroken but developing line of belief and practice they directly inherited and Protestants choosing to emphasize their 'rescuing' of neglected insights from the early Church. While the Catholics meticulously charted lines of kings, bishops and priests from St Peter onwards, the Protestants campaigned on a platform of simplicity and faithfulness to Scripture. They also pointed to a continuity of their own: those who came before them, ready to challenge popes and councils, and who were similarly persecuted by the Catholic authorities. Such a debate, though it was fierce and implacable, actually illustrates another feature of historical interpretation, and another set of twin disciplines which might help it. Neither side was necessarily wrong, but each pointed to different things. The Catholics cherished an evolutionary view of the Church, seeing in its development over time a Spirit-led process that was desirable and purposeful. It did not matter that the Church had not preserved itself in its pristine original form, because it had adapted faithfully to changed times and circumstances. In our own interpretations, this kind of evolution will always be present and, if we are reasonably confident that it was a process of integrity and faith, it need not matter. It can even be welcomed and celebrated.

Those Protestant historians, if they could only have admitted it (a few of them, usually the English ones, did), knew that this evolution was inevitable. As the Protestant churches grew and spread through Europe, they formulated practices and published new statements as the times demanded. It was impossible not to. But their histories did point to another scientific discipline in their understanding, the need to 'project' a founding, original belief into the present and allow it to clean up what had developed *unfaithfully* in the Church's life. We might think of this as an exercise in ballistics: charting the trajectory of an object directly from where it is fired to its landing site. The Protestants looked at the early Church's reliance on Scripture alone as its sole authority, and thought that this was one thing that was badly neglected in the sixteenth century. They thus tried to project that early belief into their present and allow it to correct the evolutionary process where necessary. Similarly, John Wesley felt that he rediscovered certain emphases in the early Church which were forgotten by the eighteenth century, to the Church's detriment. He thus attempted to project them directly into his own context, to correct what the evolutionary process had spoiled. The result was some of his key teachings on the possibility of perfection, the universality of God's love and his characteristic bias to the poor. Evolution and ballistics reflect the twin sciences of our historical interpretation.

If, however, it is important to bear in mind that our own interpretations can never be the last word and that we do not have the monopoly on truth, are all interpretations of our tradition equally valid? Is it impossible to make any judgements? The answer, of course, is no, but it is important to think about the criteria by which we make those judgements, just as with biblical interpretation, and those Sundays when we just do not like what the preacher says! A major part of the answer to the question about judgement would be the need to understand from where our criticism comes, by having answered those ten hermeneutical questions for ourselves. Question 9, about what it is in me to which the story 'speaks', is especially important here. We will always bring our own commitments to a reading of any faith text, be it the Bible or tradition, and understanding what in others' interpretations rubs up against our own is part of the self-discipline of awareness we talked about earlier. While making judgements about others' interpretations, though, we need also to be open to the reality out of which they speak, and their own commitments and struggles within the Christian faith. Often, all of us read and interpret faith records and texts with deliberately chosen focus and intention about the outcome. Such intentional focus is what in biblical studies is called a hermeneutical 'key': the 'lens' through which we read the historical record of our faith.

The twentieth century saw great changes in the way the Bible was read. The way in which the world suddenly became so much smaller and more accessible revolutionized our understanding of others and ourselves, and posed multiple challenges to the ways in which we practised faith. Such a transformation prompted and encouraged also a growing realization that many people had been marginalized over the centuries by their absence from scripture and Church life. As it became necessary to afford them an equal place, readings of the Bible developed which attempted to see things through the lens of their experience. So emerged ways of reading the Bible which remembered the experience of black people, the long effect of patriarchal societies on women, the part that colonialism played in enforcing Christianity on local cultures, and the presence of the poor, downtrodden and voiceless in every period of human history. Black theology, feminist theology, postcolonial theology and liberation theology are just four examples of hermeneutical keys – there are many more. One primary consideration to bear in mind when another interpretation of the Christian past jars with ours is the extent to which it simply represents a worldview, or a background or perspective, with which we are not familiar. There is an old Native American saying about the value of walking a mile in someone else's moccasins. Being open to the way others interpret the tradition of the Church – their hermeneutical 'key' – is a valuable way for us to do this. We will, in fact, be experimenting with a series of lenses, or keys, to reading our Christian history as we begin to explore particular issues in Part Two. For now, it is enough that we are open to their existence, and to the ways they can helpfully challenge us.

Even so, there remains the real possibility that we shall want to reject other representations of the past as unfaithful, or lacking Christian character and integrity. It's therefore important to conclude by thinking briefly about what guidelines should shape our interpretations. Inescapably, of course, we are children of our generation, and the way we look at the past will always be defined by the values and principles by which we live. This is what E. H. Carr meant when, quoting another historian, he observed that 'all history is contemporary history'.[11] Inevitably, we will judge others' claims about tradition by the standards and qualities which they seem to embody, and by their fidelity both to our highest aspirations and the ethical core of our faith. Sometimes, as we have seen and will see, reassessing our history involves rejecting parts of it – the Crusades, the marginalization of women – which no longer represent our beliefs. Such dark periods can still be helpful, in holding a mirror up to our current obsessions and ideologies and convicting us of persistent sins that span the generations.

We should, though, be very careful here not to fall into the trap of supposing that the passage of time always involves evolution for the better. The march of progress is very far from being as inevitable as we often imagine. The reforms of Wilberforce, the actions of Pope John XXIII and the campaigns of Martin Luther King all grew from that deep conviction, examined earlier, that something had gone rotten in the evolution of belief and practice that a return to earlier understandings could rectify. Interpreting our past, informed by reason, our experience in the present and our reading of the sacred texts of Scripture can be as much a process in renewing former glories in new forms fit for the present age as one in giving thanks for how far we have come. That is the tightrope we are constantly treading. In a generation which has witnessed unprecedented growth in weapons of mass destruction, exponential widening of the gap between the world's rich and poor, and the stubborn refusal of governments effectively to address human rights violations and impending climatic catastrophe, we should never be too smug about the place from which we start.

All that said, it is axiomatic that our interpretation of our religious past will be conditioned by the way we view our religion, and by our own sense of what is and is not authentic Christianity. It may therefore be all we can do simply to be open to the interpretations of others and to allow them to speak to and even possibly change us. Maybe we can even go a little further, and acknowledge a considerable agreement between religious and secular historians about the purpose of history. Turning to this question at the end of his study, Gaddis stresses the role of historians as those who help individuals and societies to define themselves in ways neither too oppressed by the past nor too liberated by a total ignorance of it. They create boundaries for healthy living, accountable to and rooted in what went before, but ultimately possessing the freedom of self-definition. So too, Holgate and Starr define the ultimate test of any biblical hermeneutic as that which is 'life-affirming', and which points people towards the fullness of the Kingdom of God which is coming. The World Council of Churches calls us to remember that the ways in which we interpret our Scriptures *and* our history must be consistent with 'the struggle for peace, justice and the integrity of creation, the renewed sense of mission in witness and service, [and] the liturgy in which the Church proclaims and celebrates the promise of God's reign'.[12]

In all these things, in this constant and unending work of interpretation and reinterpretation, in our holding ourselves open to the judgement of the past and judging it in our turn, in tracing both the evolution of our beliefs and the need to project our foundational principles into the realities of the contemporary world, in our laborious and yet life-giving hermeneutical duty, we are never done. Biblical scholars have long talked of the 'hermeneutical cycle', in which we have constantly to be refining and honing our understanding of ourselves, our sense of identity, purpose, character and destiny, by allowing our beliefs to meet the test of practice, and to go back to the drawing board where they fail. In all of this, too, we seek the ongoing inspiration of God's ageless Spirit, and remember the great company of those in whose footsteps we follow as we seek to make an ancient tradition relevant in our generation. The hymn-writer Brian Wren sums it up for us, speaking of our ancestors in faith:

While others bowed to changeless gods,
    They met a mystery:
God with an uncompleted name,
    'I am what I will be';
And by their tents, around their fires,
    In story, song and law,
They praised, remembered, handed on,
    A past that promised more.

From Abraham to Nazareth
    The promise changed and grew;
While some, remembering the past,
    Recorded what they knew,
And some, in letters or laments,
    In prophecy and praise,
Recovered, held, and re-expressed
    New hope for changing days.[13]

Notes

1 The view of the novelist L. P. Hartley, in *The Go-Between*.

2 On this, see also Rowan Williams, *Why Study the Past?: The Quest for the Historical Church*, London: Darton, Longman and Todd, 2005.

3 E. H. Carr, *What Is History?*, New York: Vintage, 1961, p. 32.

4 J. L. Gaddis, *The Landscape of History*, Oxford: Oxford University Press, 2002, p. 41.

5 Gaddis, *Landscape of History*, p. 48.

6 Andrew Motion, 'Remember This', in *Public Property*, London: Faber & Faber, 2002, p. 63.

7 Williams, *Why Study the Past?*, p. 97.

8 David Holgate and Rachel Starr, *Biblical Hermeneutics*, London: SCM Press, 2006, pp. 89–121.

9 Carr, *What Is History?*, p. 143.

10 B. K. Blount, 'The Last Word in Biblical Authority', in W. Brueggemann, W. C. Placher and B. K. Blount, *Struggling with Scripture*, Louisville: Westminster John Knox Press, pp. 51–69, quoted in Holgate and Starr, *Biblical Hermeneutics*, pp. 189–90.

11 Carr, *What Is History?*, p. 22.

12 Holgate and Starr, *Biblical Hermeneutics*, p. 187.

13 'Deep in the Shadows of the Past', *Hymns & Psalms* 447.

Part Two

READINGS IN TRADITION

4

NATURE'S FULL OF LOVE

Women, Sexuality and the Family

Soon after her narrow loss in the 2008 Democratic Party primary elections, United States Senator Hillary Rodham Clinton took stock of her achievement. She reflected that her mother was born, eighty years or so previously, into a country in which she, as a woman, was unable to participate in the democratic process at all. Her daughter Chelsea, however, had been able to vote for her mother as the next Head of State. Despite the surprise of her defeat and her evident disappointment, Clinton was able to take some comfort in the thought that she had put 'eighteen million cracks', equivalent to the number of votes cast for her, in the so-called 'glass ceiling', that invisible barrier to the promotion and advancement of the careers and aspirations of women.

Clinton's observation underscores dramatically the enormous changes which Western societies in particular have undergone in the last century. Women, who were previously viewed as homemakers, the property of their husbands, a 'weaker sex' constitutionally unsuited for positions of great influence or responsibility, have seen the options in personal, business and public life open up to them with extraordinary speed. As their work and contribution were made essential through times of war and national emergency, the male establishment's shared understanding about their capabilities and gifts was fatally challenged. The indefatigable, unrelenting efforts of the Suffragette and similar movements ensured that the cause of women's rights was kept at the forefront of public conversation and national debate. Though there is still progress to be made in equal pay and opportunities for women, their 'foremothers' of the 1920s would surely look in astonishment at the lives and possibilities of early twenty-first-century women.

For women of faith, this process has raised pressing questions about the role of religion in their historical subjugation. Christians see nowhere more clearly than in the history of women and the family the way in which the Church has been shaped by and dependent upon the surrounding culture in its own views. Only in the late twentieth century, as the place of women in society drastically altered, was there any move towards their ordination. Only when the prevailing mindset changed did the Church – eventually – see fit to follow suit. In fairness therefore, the diminishing of women in the life of the Church simply reflects the society in which the Church has found itself, and the Church is apparently no worse than humanity generally in this regard. Neither, however, is it any better, and here lies an issue for many, men and women alike. If the Church has been so culturally conditioned, if it has been so late in accepting the changes going on around it and adapting itself to fit them, how are we to understand it? In order to find a place as leaders in and shapers of the life of the Church, do women have to ignore the Church's history and strike out in an entirely new direction? Where 'are' they in the Church's history? Is there any way of rescuing their voice and presence in the Christian tradition, or must they simply ignore its (now thankfully outdated) oppression?

While at theological college, I was charged by one of my teachers to write an essay on the rôles of women in the early Church. I did my research, and mentioned prophetesses, house church leaders, desert mothers, mystics and those whose ministries Paul calls out for special praise in his letters. In our tutorial, my teacher asked me why I had not mentioned martyrdom: to which I replied that it didn't really seem to me that violent death was something one might find offered at a ministry fair as a rôle in the Church! The question perhaps reflects something of the narrow scope of women's options throughout the Church's history, though; and although the martyrs certainly have an honoured place in its worshipping life and collective memory, it may be that martyrdom is an increasingly attractive way to make a lasting contribution to the faith if real leadership is always denied to you.

It has never helped, of course, that many of the foundational texts of the Judaeo-Christian tradition reflect the societal bias against women in the context of which they were written. One reading of the Genesis stories makes Eve entirely to blame for humanity's depravity, who, with her feminine wiles, lured Adam into sin. Those of a more literalist mind have certainly chosen to see those early chapters, not as an 'aetiology', a story of beginnings into every detail of which we need not read too much, but rather a serious account of the flaws of women. The New Testament similarly reflects both general cultural norms and specific local issues when the limits of women's ministry are strictly defined. The First Letter to Timothy surely dates from a time later than Paul and was written by one of his followers and not the man himself; but its presence in Scripture poses serious questions for those wishing to offer women a greater voice in Church life, with its insistence that women keep quiet in worship and never assume a teaching rôle. Thus, despite Jesus' and Paul's often strikingly unusual respect for and work alongside women, the Bible has usually been another authority for their oppression.

The prejudice of a male-dominated society led to the establishment of a Christian teaching tradition that was similarly suspicious about women, in ways often bolstered by the insights and instructions of the Law about women's physiology and sexuality. Christian theology and its best-known exponents did nothing to counter society's mistrust of women and its frequent disgust around the reproductive process. Even in the

Church's understanding, the menstrual cycle was often seen as inherently unclean, and female sexuality as the rock on which many otherwise good men were shipwrecked. Indeed, many of the Church's finest minds merely encouraged such views. Saint Augustine, in the fourth century, perhaps did most to create an innate fear of sexuality generally and female sexuality in particular among Christians, in expressing his revulsion about the way in which sexual activity clouded rational thought and seemed to reflect baser human instincts from which Christians ought to be escaping as they grew in holiness. Eve increasingly became the symbol for this notion of how dangerous and corrupted a thing human sexuality had become. Augustine's teaching set the tone and defined a shared understanding for centuries to come.

Such teaching only served to underline and reinforce society's perceptions of the inferiority of women. Throughout most of human history, women have largely been regarded as the property of their families, and daughters the means to ensure the family's standing by a good marriage: the most important of tasks. Very often, this was a contract entered into at a very young age; the presentation of Juliet in Shakespeare's famous play underscores this. In love with her Romeo, the teenage Juliet attempts to resist the marriage to the nobleman Paris which her family has negotiated for her: and to safeguard their own security. Even before he knows that she is in love with the son of his mortal enemy, Capulet deals with his daughter's rebellion and youthful defiance with anger and dire threats of rejection and violence:

> Hang thee, young baggage, disobedient wretch!
> I tell thee what: get thee to church o'Thursday,
> Or never after look me in the face.
> Speak not, reply not, do not answer me.
> My fingers itch ...
> But an you will not wed, I'll pardon you!
> Graze where you will, you shall not house with me.[1]

Clearly, in such a position and viewed in such a way, women had very few chances to exercise leadership or play a formative role beyond the family. Indeed, it may be possible that the Church restricted their options even more than the prevailing culture. Historians of the medieval period, for instance, have commented that the arrival of Christianity in England in the sixth century placed women under greater curtailment than before, with its new, scriptural insistence on wives being subject to husbands and its imposition of silence on female worshippers.[2] Despite the occasional presence of strong queens leading their countries, in fact little substantially changed in the rôle and status of women in the Christian world until the movements of the twentieth century whose effects we have already seen.

Such a quick survey merely repeats what we already knew: that the Church, no less than the cultures in which it has existed, has been an institution which has viewed women as lesser mortals, with a lower status and fewer opportunities than men. The purpose of this chapter, though, is not to document that discrimination, which is widely detailed elsewhere. Rather, it is to ask the question with which we began: given this history, given the bias of the Christian tradition against women and their leadership in the Church, where are we to look for any sense of alternative voices? Where are today's new generation of women ministers, priests and bishops to look for any sense of where their sisters have been all this time? Or, to restate the alternative, is the recent change in the standing of women in the Church just a drastic rejection, whether justifiable or erroneous, of all that has gone before? Remembering the image from Chapter 1, of a 'large room' in which we may wander at will and find many divergent signs of God's presence in human life, I want to suggest that women have in fact been able to exercise considerable leadership within the Church, within the confines in which they were placed. It is sometimes necessary to search hard to find them under all the male hegemony, but they have been present: passionate, prophetic, compelling and courageous. Again, because an exhaustive catalogue is impossible, let us examine six categories through which Christian women have been able to defy the conventions of their age and shape the faith and life of the Christian Church.

Early Church pioneers

Women, it is often noted, occupied an unusually prominent place in the life and work of Jesus, and their company – and testimony – seem to have been important for him. The gradual institutionalization of the Church which grew up after him ensured that their rôle in its life was often marginal. For all that, the early Christian Scriptures contain some startling reflections on women, not least Paul's extraordinary claim that 'there is no longer male and female, for all of you are one in Christ Jesus' (Galatians 3.28). As the Church struggled to present and define itself in the face of a hostile public, the witness of women was as important as any. In times of persecution, the fortitude and courage of those brought before the authorities and even of those executed was a compelling testimony to the power of the new faith. For all my reluctance to acknowledge the martyrs, in fact accounts of their sufferings and determined faith were highly influential in the early Church. An anonymous account survives of the deaths of two such women, Perpetua and Felicitas, in the year 203. Their dignity, bravery and trust in God are emphasized by the author, who describes their endurance of imprisonment and questioning before their very public executions. Perpetua takes care to cover her nakedness and keep her hair tied up through her ordeal, a sign of her modesty and integrity, while Felicitas actually gives birth during her captivity. It was of such 'great women' as these that the theologian Tertullian wrote when he described the blood of martyrs as the 'seed' of Christianity's growth.

There soon developed in the early Church a quest for deeper spirituality and a more earnest desire for holiness and the life of prayer. Led by heroes such as St Antony, more and more

Christians took to the loneliness of the deserts. There, they did battle with demons both inside and out, and sought, through harsh abstinence and demanding discipline, the ideal of closeness to God. In time, such seekers after God banded together in communities distant from urban distractions, and the monastic life was slowly created. While their efforts and biographies seem strange to modern people, these rigorous individuals made a huge impact on the Church, and fostered an emphasis on spiritual practice that still profoundly affects us. Interestingly, there were among these 'Desert Fathers' also 'Desert Mothers', whose wisdom, authority and sanctity were no less revered. The wisdom of women like Ama (a word simply meaning 'mother'), Sarah and Ama Syncletica in the fifth century was gathered into the collections of desert writings which became popular resources for spiritual directors and seekers in those formative early centuries. From her experience in the desert, Syncletica encouraged more everyday Christians to cultivate a life of reflection, advising, 'You can be a solitary in your mind even when you live in the middle of a crowd'.[3]

The presence of women as leaders in the early Church is often obscured, because the men who wrote the first histories of the Church tended to write from their own perspective, and marginalize the contribution of women. For all that, their influence was often critical. It remains an intriguing and yet frustrating mystery to discern exactly what role was played by the women referred to by Paul as leaders in the Church – Phoebe, Mary, Julia, the sister of Nereus, Lois, Eunice and others. Powerful, royal women affected the growth of Christianity in better-documented ways. Helena, the mother of the Emperor Constantine, exercised great influence, both in the practice of the faith across the empire and in her inculcation of Christian belief in her son, under whose rule Christianity escaped persecution by becoming the empire's official religion. Helena is perhaps the most prominent woman leader in the early Church; but, at lower levels of power, we are given many glimpses of the leadership and wisdom of women. Although such glimpses reflect a male bias in the recording of history, they also offer some basis for tracing the presence and importance of women in the Church even from its earliest days.

Religious

From the Desert Mothers like Syncletica onwards, women were as involved in the growth of the monastic movement as men. Orders of religious communities for women have existed for almost as long as those for men, and have based their common life on the same foundational rules and texts. As time passed, these religious communities became important centres of the local economy and an essential focus of social provision and Christian piety. By the medieval period, entering a religious order actually became one of the few ways in which women were able to exercise a role of leadership within Church or society. While very few, of course, were ever able to aspire to becoming an abbess, or leader of a convent or nunnery, those who did were often formidable and influential figures in their own right. They are those to whom modern women often look for inspiration and some sense of the presence of female authority in an age which generally forbade such a thing.

A few examples will illustrate the importance of such women. The seventh century saw a great blossoming of religious orders and institutions in England, and some of the greatest leaders of this movement were women. Hilda of Whitby established several monastic communities in the north, and was famous as a woman of sanctity, learning, courage and wisdom. She was a patron of poetry, a widely sought-after spiritual guide, and exercised a critical influence in the formation of Christianity in the British Isles through her involvement in the Synod of Whitby, which determined the form of the faith which was to be practised. Etheldreda of Ely, similarly, devoted her life to the foundation of religious houses, and the cathedral at Ely which was described in Chapter 1 remains her greatest legacy. Etheldreda had to fight hard and against immense family pressure to resist the expectations and conventions of her time and devote herself to Christian leadership. She even denied her long-suffering husband, King Egfrith of Northumbria, the pleasures of the marriage bed: which may in fact have eventually persuaded him to release her to her religious vocation so that he could marry a less fastidious woman. Both Hilda and Etheldreda were from royal families, which afforded them opportunities usually denied to those of lower birth: but, nevertheless, their courage and their achievements were equally significant.

Their spirit, too, was reborn in some significant women pioneers of religious orders in later generations. Clare of Assisi fought hard against the male hierarchy of the Church in order to found a female order based on the rule of Saint Francis, her friend, mentor and guide. She was eventually to learn of the Pope's granting of her wish on her deathbed in 1253. The Poor Clares, as they became known, exercised a great influence in the shaping of popular piety, equal in many ways to that of their male counterparts, the Franciscans. Three centuries later, Teresa of Avila faced a similarly uphill struggle in following her vocation to the establishing of Catholic religious communities for women during the upheaval of the Protestant Reformation. Her personal journal describes her humility in the face of her superiors' resistance, but also her fierce determination to persist and her willingness to exercise guile and cunning in order to work around the seemingly immovable obstacle of male complacency and control. Teresa's work, writings and spiritual wisdom have profoundly influenced centuries of Christians, male and female, ever since. Bernini's sculpture of her 'ecstasy', in Rome, remains one of the most iconic depictions of mystical spiritual experience in the world. Something of Teresa's passion, humility, spiritual depth and political astuteness can be seen in later female pioneers, and perhaps even in her twentieth-century namesake Mother Teresa, whose extraordinary work in the slums of Calcutta was made possible by her possession of similar qualities – and even a similar need to be assertive when the men at the top were resistant.

The Beguines

The Beguines represent an intriguing case study of the way in which some medieval women may have taken authority into their own hands, to live out their faith and their life as they wished, against the culture of the day. Ursula King describes how they have even been described as 'feminists before their time'.[4] Little is known of them, but the picture that has so far emerged is fascinating. The Beguines were lay women, who lived together, in communities or in scattered but connected houses of a few women, and devoted themselves to prayer, to the care of the poor and needy, and often to the description of their spiritual experiences in writing. They shared common aims, but generally resisted creating a monastic rule of life. It seems that some European cities contained large Beguine populations: Cologne boasted 100 houses and 1,000 Beguines between 1250 and 1350; Strasbourg by the fifteenth century had 600 of these extraordinary women. Beguine groups spread into Germany, France, the Low Countries and even to England. They were entirely self-sufficient.

Not surprisingly, the details of the life of such counter-cultural medieval women are scarcely recorded, because of the perspective of the men writing the history of the time. We can only speculate about the consequences of the decisions made by these women, and about how their families may have felt about their refusal to follow the normal course of marriage and child-bearing, in order to join a female religious commune. Something of their intense love for God and their fierce passion to serve God and neighbour in common life with others is conveyed in their writings. The Beguines have sometimes been called 'women troubadours of God', because of the extraordinary language of their writings, emphasizing intimacy with God in the style and language of courtly love poetry. Women such as Mechtild of Magdeburg and Hadewijch of Brabant exemplify this movement. Another, Marguerite Porete, shows the dangers to which the Beguine authors were exposed: her work was condemned and publicly burned by her bishop, before she herself was imprisoned and executed for heresy in 1310. Marguerite's sin was too confidently to espouse an independence of mind and life, which conflicted with the authority of the institutional Church. She and her sister Beguines also belong to a larger category of influential women, to whom we turn next.

The mystics

Mysticism is a phenomenon common to all religions, and the mystics represent a diverse and varied group. It is, however, interesting to note how many of Christianity's most influential and important mystics have been women, often in times when a woman's ability to exercise leadership in any other way was extremely limited. Mystics are hard to define, but, generally speaking, are those who have an intense, deeply personal experience of God, and whose spiritual lives are particularly deep and well developed. They are often granted visions, or feel that they have been given insights or revelations directly from God. Their presence in all world religions can be a source of tension as well as benefit, because of the very individualistic nature of their faith, which can sometimes seem to clash with inherited creeds or fixed beliefs. When mystics can escape these dangers, however, they are frequently highly in demand as spiritual directors, confessors and faith guides.

One such was Mother Julian of Norwich, who lived as a recluse and hermit around 1350–1423. Julian is perhaps the best-known Christian mystic, whose gentle, reassuring visions of God's inclusivity, love and care of all creation have ensured her a place in the Christian imagination to the present day. Julian spoke of God, and Jesus, as fulfilling the role of mother as well as father, and so enabled deeper and richer reflection on the divine person and character. Her distinctive theology and style have given rise in the present to 'Julian' groups which meet for meditation, reflection and prayer. It is perhaps extraordinary to consider how such an isolated life has, through its commitment, wisdom and deep spiritual dedication, exercised so profound an influence on subsequent generations of Christians. Yet Julian's life and works were, for many years after her death, little known or celebrated until their rediscovery two centuries later. These days, Julian takes her place among and may be said to be representative of a great number of ground-breaking women mystics of many ages and times, whose life of prayer and imaginative response to faith have offered Christians new ways of thinking, praying and believing: Hildegard of Bingen, Catherine of Siena, Jeanne de Chantal, Evelyn Underhill, Edith Stein, Simone Weil.[5] We shall be encountering some of them in subsequent chapters, because their voice is so frequently one which offers the Church, from within, a corrective to or a fresh perspective on some of its most difficult issues and some of its deepest errors.

Reformers

There have been, throughout the Church's history, constant movements of renewal, reform and change, either focused on the Church itself or the wider society of which it is a part. Some of those who have contributed most to such movements have been women, finding within the Christian tradition the challenge and demand to make a difference. We have already glimpsed the work of monastic reformers like Hilda and Teresa of Avila, and those, like Mother Teresa, who have challenged such injustices as humanity's treatment of the poor. Scattered throughout Christian history we find other examples of strong female leadership in reforming the Church or seeking a fairer world. Prominent among the former we might mention Queen Elizabeth I of England, who rose to great power purely on account of the accident of her noble birth, but whose wisdom, insight, courage and iron determination led not only to the adoration of her people as a protector of their shores but also to the admiration of subsequent generations, who have judged her a key creator and enforcer of a religious settlement in England whose genius has survived the test of passing time. The Church of England and, by extension, the global Anglican Communion owe their character and unique combination of theological emphases and practices to nothing so much as her own tenacity and authority, as well as her desire to move her people into a period of greater stability and harmony than they had experienced in the years of her father's, brother's and sister's rules.

As subjects and citizens too, Christian women have been equally well represented as the makers of change. The eighteenth-century fight to end the slave trade in the British Empire was ably aided by a number of gifted women, whose contributions are often unjustly eclipsed by those of more famous men. The Baptist, Martha Gurney, used her publishing house to print key documents highlighting the reality of slavery; the remarkable Mary Morris Knowles, a Quaker, used her experience as an early advocate of women's rights to join the fight for abolition by arguing for abstention from slave products. She was thus a pioneer of the 'Fair trade' movement, and raised up other campaigners to follow her, such as her good friend Jane Harry Thresher. A few decades later, Elizabeth Fry devoted her life to campaigning for penal reform, shocked at what she experienced as a prison visitor, and motivated by her faith convictions to remember the cause of the prisoner, the hungry and the homeless. The society she founded in 1817 to be the voice of her work was the first national women's organization in Britain, and she maintained her work even in the face of fierce criticism that she was neglecting her duty to family by such activity. It is not hard to see in these women the kind of bravery, conscience and Christian ethic that later animated Harriet Tubman, Rosa Parks and Coretta Scott-King in their leading roles in the fight for the abolition of slavery and the equal treatment of African-Americans in the USA.

The feminist movement

Just as the diminishment of women in the Church's life has been a reflection of their status in society generally, so too the gradual opening of the opportunities available to them has re-flected seismic shifts in culture and public discourse. Drawing on the influence of early pioneers like Knowles, the feminists of the 1960s onwards demanded and eventually made possible huge changes in the standing and position of women. The work of feminist theologians has been similarly important in alter-ing the Church's understanding of women and their place in leadership. One aspect of that shift has been to 'rediscover' the presence of some of the women we have just encountered in the life and history of the Church, and to realize their im-portance and the ways in which their work has shaped subse-quent centuries. All this work has enabled many churches in recent decades to face the most divisive question of all, and to contemplate the overturning of centuries of practice and the clear teaching of at least one passage of Scripture by ordaining women to pastorate and priesthood. Such a revision, although it has offended many who hold to the need to preserve practice unaltered through the ages, has nevertheless been founded on an attempt to be faithful to the wider Christian tradition and the message of other scriptures. Indeed, it has relied upon the kind of careful historical hermeneutics already outlined.

The purpose of feminist theology and its outworking in the Church's life are clearly summarized by one of its best and most widely known scholars, Rosemary Radford Ruether, in this description of her own and the movement's hermeneutical key:

The critical principle of feminist theology is the promotion of the full humanity of women. Whatever denies, diminishes, or distorts the full humanity of women is, therefore, ap-praised as not redemptive. Theologically speaking, whatever diminishes or denies the full humanity of women must be presumed not to reflect the divine or an authentic relation to the divine, or to reflect the authentic nature of things, or to be the authentic work of an authentic redeemer or a com-munity of redemption.

Ruether goes on to note that the 'full humanity of women' has not existed in history, except in affirming itself in 'limited and subversive ways', such as those we have already described. In those ways, though – and in those earlier pioneers of this view – she argues that modern women may glimpse their redemption and their call to begin to 'imagine a world without sexism'.[6] Her work most eloquently and passionately describes the need for the kind of work in which we are engaged here, of paying attention to *all* the voices in the household of faith, and seeking to be faithful to tradition in its broadest sense as we seek to make similarly faithful responses to the modern world. It is not fanciful for modern Christian women to sense themselves numbered among a great crowd of witnesses and surrounded by sisters from every age and time, as they witness to the fullness of what Ruether called 'an alternative social order demanded by obedience to God'.

Sexuality and the family

The twentieth century has also been remarkable for the speed with which society has become more accepting and even affirming of those whose sexualities and lifestyles were previously the object of fear and contempt. While it was illegal to be a practising homosexual in England just 50 years ago, same-sex couples are now able to enter civil partnerships and enjoy the same legal rights and benefits as heterosexual ones. Amid this extraordinary pace of change, the Church has been as affected as it was over the role of women. The debates which regularly divide the churches about the place of gay men and lesbians in their congregations and among their clergy are conducted with no less intensity than those over the ordination of women. Indeed, as the Anglican Communion has discovered, they have the potential to split the Church entirely. That homosexuality is now an orientation which can be publicly and freely owned, and that gay people no longer need to hide themselves in shame, has profoundly challenged the Church's understanding of the issue. The presence of those gay people, both open and closeted, in churches makes it an urgent pastoral and missiological issue as well. As with the move to ordain women, those opposed to the full integration of gay men and lesbians (as well as bisexuals and transgendered people) into the Church's life always assert that the practice of homosexuality has, from Paul onwards, been declared to be incompatible with Christianity. The argument from tradition, in other words, seems to be very strong.

This approach needs more careful study and not a little unpicking. It is not the case, in the first place, that the experience of gay people is always unarticulated in the Church's history from among the faithful. More basically, too, the arguments against the full inclusion of gays and lesbians often rest on false suppositions about what is *thought* to have been the universal and continual teaching of the Church. It is actually a debate which affects the whole of Christian teaching on sexuality, marriage and family life. What the tradition reveals is a Church constantly adapting to fit societal practice, not the other way round, and refining and even flatly changing its theology to do so. Gay people, like women, have also been able to find some fairly authoritative voices hidden in the Christian tradition which seem to articulate their deepest longings and desires, and their demand for their sincere faith to be given respect. As we investigate this area, we will therefore examine both the ways in which modern understandings of marriage and sexuality by no means represent an unbroken line of thought from the early Church, and the ways in which, at some times in the Christian tradition, the articulation of same-sex attraction has been thought entirely normal and honourable. In all this, we need to pay attention to the hermeneutical process and be aware both of ways in which Church teaching must change to be faithful to new circumstances and human realities, and of ways in which such change can still be faithful to the past by being attentive both to the context of previous teaching and to the hidden voices in the conversation over many centuries.

In considering the ways in which the Church formed its views about the proper role of women in its life, we noted how its understanding of sexuality itself, as an innate human trait, has been shaped by powerful voices whose influence, in that area at least, is now rather less strong. As recently as the 1960s, the Roman Catholic Church found itself involved in a storm of debate about contraception; Pope Paul VI's teaching that it was still prohibited for Catholics in good standing gravely disappointed those who had seen in him and in his handling of the Second Vatican Council hope for a faith more in tune with the lives of ordinary Catholics. It may seem strange that contraception should be so controversial. The Pope's teaching, though, was based on those very views about sex and sexuality which can be traced back to Saint Augustine, and to the early Church's evolving sense that celibacy and virginity were the most blessed states in which to live, because unblemished by engagement in acts of lust or passion. It was Augustine who formulated that view into the teaching that sex was only ever to be engaged in as a means to produce children. Even then, he believed, sex was still sinful, but something of a necessary evil for the continuation of human life. Any kind of sex that did not have that aim – and potential – was, he said, beyond forgiveness: for instance, with a woman known to be infertile, or past the menopause, or sex in which there was the intent to prevent fertilization in any way or by any means. Later theologians thus came to call this kind of sex the 'sin against nature', a term often and misleadingly cited only against homosexual activity and partnerships, which were at best on the fringes of its original intent.

On the question of 'the joy of sex', Augustine thought that the fact it was pleasurable represented a sure sign of its sinfulness. He had lived for many years before his conversion with a mistress, so he might have thought he knew what he was talking about. The Church, at least at the highest levels, agreed with him for many centuries. More recently, however, the Catholic Church has come to allow that sex might, after

97

all, be a gift of a loving God and not merely the prime evidence of our fallen state. It's fairly clear that there have always been individual Christian thinkers and writers who have celebrated sexuality as a gift; only in recent years has that been articulated more generally and positively by the churches as institutions. However, once that admission is made, it is hard to understand how the old prohibitions on non-procreative sex can remain. The whole basis of Augustine's argument was that, because sex was both symptom of and driver towards sin, it should be as infrequent an activity as possible: indeed, only undertaken when it was imperative for the propagation of the species. Take away that view of it, and everything else changes too. In addition, modern crises over diseases which previous generations could scarcely have imagined ought also to demand a re-evaluation of traditional teaching on this. It seems a sin of a different kind to forbid contraception while the AIDS epidemic in Africa claims millions of lives every year. The past has a vote: not a veto. Nor does it speak in flat monotones, but rather sings with rich harmonies in which all the lines must be heard.

The sanctity of marriage, and the Church's consistency of teaching about it, is another key argument of those opposed to same-sex partnerships. In fact, the Church's teaching about marriage has been subject to constant evolution over the years, as it has adapted to a changing understanding in society more generally. In this, it is interesting to note that earlier generations of Christians were perhaps more able and willing to engage in the hermeneutical process than recent ones. The tradition itself does not show evidence of a single, unbending, concept of marriage which has refused to alter with the years, but rather a willingness to employ previous ideas in new ways as the times demanded. Indeed, marriage is in some ways an institution which the Church has increasingly 'stolen' from society and made all its own. Marriage in various forms was, of course, common in many places and cultures before the arrival of Christianity. Only in 1215 did the Church rule that it was a sacrament: in other words, a rite which publicly claimed and enacted God's hidden blessing on those entering it. At the Reformation, of course, Protestants rejected this interpretation, while still according it a great honour as God's way for man and woman to live together.

The Church was equally happy for many hundreds of years to accept the idea that a marriage contract needed only the consent of the two parties to be legally binding. Only as late as the sixteenth century and the Council of Trent did the Catholic Church decide that a priest needed to be present at a marriage ceremony. More important than the ceremony itself was the preparatory decision-making about whom one should marry, a process in which the Church sanctioned the customs generally prevalent around it. In the first place, as we have seen, women were only very recently granted much influence in the choosing of a marriage partner, and before that were viewed and treated as one of the family's most useful possessions in the strengthening of alliances, the generation of wealth and the preservation of the family line. Intermarriage between races was a horrific notion to most Western societies until very recently; the Church has certainly played its role in promulgating the view that such a thing is 'revolting, disgraceful and almost bestial' and in supporting anti-miscegenation laws. Over time, the whole definition of family life has changed, from seeing husband and wife as co-labourers bound together for the purpose of making a living and staying alive, to the greater emphasis on emotional attachment with which modern people are more familiar. It is certainly important to know that the ideal of the nuclear family to which we aspire and to which social conservatives appeal was largely an invention of the nineteenth century. Previously, it was thought to be beneficial if a couple could admire and even like each other, but by no means essential, provided that life could go on, children be produced and the family flourish. Nor is the permanence of marriage any more of an ancient idea: divorce was absolutely banned only in the sixteenth century, as the Catholics responded fiercely to the Protestants' sense that *some* acts of infidelity warranted the dissolution of the vows.[7]

Against this changing backdrop, and the Church's response to it, the issue of homosexuality has, unsurprisingly, been viewed differently at different times. So too, as the perception of same-sex relationships has altered, has the Church's predominant attitude. Christianity contains in its foundational texts, of course, some apparently strong denunciations of homosexual activity. These are fully discussed in other books, but it should be noted that the letter to the Romans in particular reflects a very Jewish disgust towards all Gentile forms of sexual behaviour, not just homosexuality, and uses such acts only as a prelude to a declaration of the sins of all humanity, Jew and Gentile. Equally, the Scriptures contain some very touching images, such as 'the disciple Jesus loved' enjoying an intimacy with and closeness to Jesus in a way that would surely raise eyebrows if witnessed by many modern Christians.[8] The uses made of these texts by subsequent generations has been varied, and dependent largely upon the prevailing culture. In understanding all of this, modern Christians will need the skills of hermeneutics previously described, to distinguish universal truth from an interpretation purely for the moment.

Still, the Church's opinions about homosexuality seem at first look to have been fairly consistent over 2,000 years. Are there hidden voices in the tradition here too? The late John Boswell, through painstaking research, was able to assert that there are. A historical scholar specializing in the medieval period, Boswell traced both the prevailing attitudes towards same-sex affection and behaviour and the ways in which the Church reflected them in its life and teaching. He discovered that 'as late as the eleventh and twelfth centuries, there appears to be no conflict between a Christian life and homosexuality. Gay life is everywhere in the art, poetry, music, history, etc. of [these] centuries ... [and] clerics were at the forefront of this revival of the gay culture'.[9] Soon after, around 1150, intolerance of such behaviour sharply increased, for reasons Boswell was never able to explain fully. He did note, however, interestingly, that this was also a period in which hatred towards Jews, Muslims and 'witches' was suddenly on the rise, and women were denied even such positions of responsibility as had previously been open to them.

For evidence, Boswell drew on the writings of some medieval saints which included beautiful evocations of same-sex love and attraction. At the time, monastic communities were the context for most scholarly activity and the centres from which writings of all kinds emerged, including poetry as well as theological works. One of the most extraordinary of such communities in the early medieval period was that which grew up around the court of King Charlemagne in the eighth century. Charlemagne presided over a great renewing of theological and literary life in his vast European kingdom, and was the first ruler to be given the title 'Holy Roman Emperor', as the Church in Rome sought greater protection from and influence over secular government. Alcuin was a scholar brought by Charlemagne from England as a key figure and leader in this intellectual effort. He gathered around himself a group of male pupils at the royal palace in Aachen, and the school became one of the foremost centres of learning in Europe. What is striking to modern ears is the language with which Alcuin referred to his students. He employs pet names for them; he uses classical allusions to indicate his feelings of affection for them; he even speaks openly of his love for some of them. The tone is tender and intimate, and apparently entirely in keeping with the conventions of the day. His evocation of deep same-sex friendship and love is timeless in its expression:

> All joys are changed into sad mournings,
> Nothing is permanent, everything will pass.
> Let me therefore flee to you with my whole heart,
> And do you flee to me from the vanishing world.[10]

Alcuin went on to become Abbot of the great monastery at Tours, where he died. He is still commemorated as one of medieval Christianity's greatest scholars and monastic leaders.

Aelred (1110–67) was the abbot of Rievaulx, a Cistercian monastery in Yorkshire, and an adviser to King Henry II. In his writings, he spoke much about friendship and love, describing his own attraction to and relationships with other boys in his youth. After entering monastic life and taking a vow of celibacy, Aelred continued to celebrate affectionate, intimate same-sex friendships as an ideal of communal life and spiritual growth. He described younger monks with whom he had developed loving relationships, without ever seeming to feel the need to express disgust about it. He even suggested that physical expression of such relationships could yield much benefit. Most moving of all perhaps were his own reflections on Jesus and John (whom he took to be 'the disciple Jesus loved'), and his thought that the example of their intimacy – which he called a 'heavenly marriage' – should be a great example to all who sought a soul mate, one 'to whom you can be united in the intimate embrace of the most sacred love'.[11] As with Alcuin, there is no sense in his writing that he was expressing anything at odds with the views of the time, nor any indication that he felt any need to keep such thoughts to himself, as shameful or abnormal. Within a very few years of his death, though, the culture changed.

The move in Western Europe towards the model of the nuclear family shifted drastically the contexts in which young people had been accustomed to live and be together. During the medieval period, groups of unmarried men and women had lived and socialized together within the great houses of their rich and influential patrons; the clerical writers whose accounts are the only written records we possess of their communal life casually record that homosexual activity was a routine and tolerable response to their youthful urges and their separated existence.[12] Increasingly, it subsequently became more common for children to stay in their smaller family units until marriage. Even so, the expression of same-sex friendship, even in quite intimate ways, has only recently become a thing to be viewed with suspicion or even disgust, in ways which reveal the often grotesque moral posturing of our times. For clergy, this depth of friendship was frequently particularly important, even into the modern period. Recent controversy concerning the great Victorian churchman and cardinal, John Henry Newman, reflects the issue. The Vatican is currently in the process of declaring him a saint: the process of canonization. One stage of that process is usually to exhume the remains of the would-be saint and place them in a church building for veneration. Newman's own grave, at his express wish, was shared with another man, Ambrose St John, a fellow priest who had been Newman's dearest friend, closest confidant and constant companion for over thirty years. The cardinal described their relationship, in its commitment and affection, as akin to that in the Old Testament between Ruth and Naomi. The order to exhume Newman's remains therefore aroused anger at this violation of his own desires – until it was discovered that he had been buried in a wooden coffin and that no remains existed. It also drew new attention to the depth and intimacy of the friendship between him and St John, and the extent to which such a bond was entirely free of negative associations and moral suspicion, even in the mid-nineteenth century. Newman said of his reaction to St John's death in 1875: 'I have ever thought no bereavement was equal to that of a husband's or wife's, but I feel it difficult to believe that any can be greater, or any one's sorrow greater, than mine'.[13]

The twentieth-century Church finds itself in quite new territory in attempting to deal with same-sex love. On the one hand, there is a strong pressure to conform to certain models of family life or gender characteristics. There is a greater attention to, and even obsession about, sexual expression and more public curiosity about 'who's sleeping with whom', a prurience easily satisfied by reference to tabloid newspapers and other media outlets which are only too happy to help, no matter how despicable the invasion of privacy. There is a culture of suspicion around sexuality and its expression which is perhaps as great as at any other time. On the other hand, as already noted, our understanding about sexual orientation is rapidly and drastically changing: scientific evidence increasingly indicates that it is genetically fixed and not a 'choice'; the law is gradually beginning to recognize same-sex unions and offer protection to those wishing to enter them; the presence of gay couples living openly together and contributing to the life of local communities has altered for ever the way they are perceived. The Church, needless to say, struggles to adapt to such rapid social change, and has itself become deeply divided as it seeks to do so. As James Alison says, the heart of the problem is the need to acknowledge a social reality unprecedented in any other place or time:

> The very fact that we have started to notice that there is something called 'the closet' is because of a comparative novelty in our history: people who have started to say 'I just am gay, or lesbian. It's not that big a deal. You can heap on me what you will, but it does no good, since I'd rather be dead than pretend.'[14]

The 2003 election of Gene Robinson, an openly gay and partnered priest, to be Bishop of the Episcopal Diocese of New Hampshire, embodied this change most dramatically. The global Anglican Communion is still dealing with the fall-out.

It may be possible, even on the basis of such a brief survey, to offer some reflections about the place and value of tradition in this argument. First, the case so often made by Christians against same-sex partnerships rests on an inaccurate and often lazy view of tradition. It claims that the Christian tradition has always been entirely uniform and consistent on the issue, and that is simply not so. Indeed, although the Roman Catholic Church has always forbidden same-sex activity, the description of same-sex attraction as an 'objective disorder' is extremely recent and would have been categorically denied in many previous generations, even by theologians. It is on this description that much recent Vatican teaching rests, and it blatantly disregards the unanimous opinion of reputable psychiatrists and psychologists. Within the Christian tradition, though, there are clear, eloquent voices which talk about deep and intimate same-sex friendships as enriching, wholesome and even Christ-like. Some of them even undermine contemporary Christian rhetoric about the sinfulness of sexual activity between those of the same gender. Second, the idea that the Church's understanding has never changed similarly needs challenging. On the whole spectrum of issues related to marriage, the family and human sexuality, the Church has clearly and frequently altered and refined its teaching to reflect shifts in contemporary attitudes and societal practices. What matters – what has always mattered – in that response is not a crude determination never to change a thing, but rather the kind of process we envisaged in Chapter 3, attentive to hermeneutical questions in both Scripture and tradition, and to human experience. To reject that understanding is in fact a far more serious denial of Christian tradition and the way it has been constantly evolving through the ages, while striving to remain faithful to its central insights about the God revealed in Christ.

Those who make the claim that the Church needs always to stand apart from the world and proclaim an unchanging social message should be more attentive to this. Otherwise, they will paint themselves into a corner of being forced to argue for the right of men to take multiple wives, for the renewal of slavery and for the complete re-subjugation of women in marriage, Church and the workplace. James Alison points to the important Catholic teaching against 'actualization': the crucial need to avoid 'reading ancient texts as referring in a straightforward way to modern realities'.[15] This is the historical fundamentalism warned against in earlier chapters. In biblical terms, for example, this would mean not reading into John 8 a denunciation of all contemporary Jews as children of the devil. Such a warning should equally be carried into our reading of history and the Christian tradition; only by carefully asking the hermeneutical questions already described can modern Christians avoid the grave error of anachronistically assuming that ancient, or medieval, or early modern, or Victorian attitudes were either uniform or identical, and that they can be easily and rightly imposed on the present.

Pastorally speaking, it is crucial that modern gay and lesbian Christians know that their orientation and even its expression finds advocates from within the tradition. For many years, the Church was at least indifferent to and sometimes even accepting of same-sex attraction and love. In that, and in its intolerance, it has reflected changes in society and cultural shifts in values. However, beneath that inconsistency there can be said to lie a deeper consistency, rooted in an understanding of the love of God revealed in Christ, which breaks down barriers, widens the scope of the covenant and celebrates all genuine human love as reflecting divine love. Gay men, lesbians and those of all gender and sexual identities may find, as women did in their struggle for equality, that they are surprised by the depth, variety and beauty of the Christian voice through the centuries. To that end, we conclude with the words of two archbishops, the first from medieval France, appointed to the post without his clear and openly expressed homosexual orientation being a factor against him. 'It is not we who teach God how to love', he declared, 'but he who taught us. He made our natures full of love.' Centuries later, Archbishop Rowan Williams, a man more caught in the crosshairs of this debate than almost any other, explicitly referring to both heterosexual and same-sex relationships, wrote:

To be formed in our humanity by the loving delight of another is an experience whose contours we can identify most clearly and hopefully if we have also learned or are learning about being the object of the causeless loving delight of God, being the object of God's love for God through incorporation into the community of God's Spirit and the taking-on of the identity of God's child.[16]

Notes

1 *Romeo and Juliet*, Act 3, Scene 5, ll. 160–4, 188–9.

2 See, for example, Helen Jewell's *Women in Medieval England*, Manchester: Manchester University Press, 1996, p. 45.

3 Quoted by Rowan Williams in *Silence and Honey Cakes: The Wisdom of the Desert*, Oxford: Lion, 2004, p. 94.

4 Ursula King, *Christian Mystics: Their Lives and Legacies throughout the Ages*, London: Routledge, 2001, p. 89.

5 Ursula King's *Christian Mystics* is easily the best and most accessible short introduction to this subject.

6 Rosemary Radford Ruether, *Sexism and God-Talk*, quoted in Joel Harrington (ed.), *A Cloud of Witnesses*, Boston: Houghton Mifflin, 2001, p. 509.

7 For more on these arguments, see, for example, A. J. Graff's accessible and incisive *What Is Marriage For?*, Boston: Beacon Press, 1999; miscegenation quotation is from p. 157.

8 John 13.23.

9 'The Church and the Homosexual: A Historical Perspective' (lecture given in 1979 and available at <www.fordham.edu/halsall/pwh/1979Boswell.html>). Boswell's use of the word 'gay' has been criticized as anachronistic by his critics; but it reflected his sense of the continuity of homosexual orientation as a fixed state of being, and the need for a culture in which it could be celebrated.

10 John Boswell, *Christianity, Social Tolerance and Homosexuality*, Chicago: University of Chicago Press, 1980, pp. 189–91.

11 Boswell, *Christianity, Social Tolerance and Homosexuality*, pp. 221–6.

12 See George Duby (ed.), *A History of Private Life*, Vol. 2, *Revelations of the Medieval World*, Cambridge, Mass.: Harvard University Press, 1988, pp. 79–81.

13 See also Ian Ker, *John Henry Newman*, Oxford: Oxford University Press, 1988, pp. 694–5.

14 James Alison, *Undergoing God*, New York: Continuum, 2006, p. 210.

15 Alison, *Undergoing God*, p. 125.

16 Boswell does not name his source, but it is probably Archbishop Ralph of Tours; Rowan Williams, *The Body's Grace*, London: LGCM, 1989, p. 9.

5

JUSTICE TOO LONG
DELAYED

Violence, the Poor and the Earth

On 26 April 1998, Bishop Juan Gerardi was found murdered in his garage in Guatemala City. His killers were as efficient as they were ruthless, and his brutal death generated a huge outpouring of anger and grief across the country. Bishop Gerardi was killed just two days after the release of a report *Guatemala: Never Again*, over whose publication he had presided. It had, for the first time, described the genocide which had been perpetrated in Guatemala during the course of a 36-year-long civil war, and had laid the blame for the deaths of hundreds of thousands of Guatemalans squarely at the door of the army and the government. Bishop Gerardi knew that his report would be controversial, and he was aware of the dangers he faced in unmasking the corruption, wickedness and murderous intent of the authorities. After his death, he was almost immediately hailed by Guatemalans as a martyr and national hero. Like his more famous and more senior colleague in El Salvador, Oscar Romero, Gerardi has come to represent the best of the Church's witness to the world: an unrelenting and courageous seeker of truth who refused to back down or back away from confrontation with the powerful and who spoke in God's name for those who had no voice and no access to justice.

Yet Bishop Gerardi's story also demonstrated a darker aspect of the Church's life and behaviour. At the time of his death, he was not running a diocese but rather acting as a parish priest in the city. As Bishop of the El Quiché diocese, he had closed down every diocesan church in 1980 as a protest against the murder of 36 local people and an attempt on his own life; when he subsequently attempted to return to Guatemala after a visit to Rome, he was denied entry and forced into an agonizing three-year exile in Costa Rica. His trip to Rome had been a deliberate – and successful – effort to enlist the support of Pope John Paul II, and it was necessary because of the intense pressure to which leaders like Gerardi and Romero were often subjected from the church's hierarchy in the Vatican. Siding with the poor, criticizing the powerful and loudly demanding justice were not always popular strategies for these bishops; frequently their actions were denounced as 'communist' and dangerously subversive by their superiors. Even John Paul himself had been lukewarm about the choices which had led inexorably to Archbishop Romero's assassination in March 1980. In Central America, the Church found itself caught between powerful regimes on the one side, often backed by Western governments, which tortured and killed their people, and the victims themselves on the other, who were to be found every Sunday in the pews of parish churches everywhere. It was an uncomfortable position and, despite the bravery of heroes like Gerardi, there were plenty of examples too of compromise and even silence, as the Church strove to protect its influence and status.

For many, Bishop Gerardi's story is representative of the whole history of the Church: despite the presence of noble, holy individuals, it is predominantly a sad record of doing deals with the powerful at the cost of integrity, and a testament to the absolute corrupting effect of worldly influence. We have already noted in passing some of the evils perpetrated by the Church in its history, and they will be our concern in this chapter: Crusades, persecution, anti-Semitism and intolerance.

So too, though, will be some of the more hidden strands, the women and men who, like Bishop Gerardi and Archbishop Romero, have re-engaged with their Christian heritage and discovered deeper and more compelling voices than the all-too-human ones which have led to violence and compromise. Further, whenever we make judgements about the past, it is important to try and place actions in their right context, and not expect from historical figures choices of which they would have been incapable. Finally, where evil clearly remains, and has been perpetrated, we need to allow history's witness to convict us too and to cast its shadow over the present. For all our sense of and confidence in human progress, the past often reveals to us how little we have learned. As we examine some of these issues, then, the need is always to be attentive: to hidden voices, to the social context of past wrongs, and to the judgement to which they still subject us, in our own time.

Living as a member of an oppressed people in an occupied nation, Jesus left few instructions for later followers who would exercise secular power about a Christian ethic and programme for doing so. His fiercest confrontations were with religious leaders, and his dealings with rulers like Herod and Pilate were minimal and reveal little in the way of a political agenda. The earliest Christians, too, had little sense that their faith in Jesus could ever have a defining or shaping effect at a national or political level. The first generation of believers thought that his return would happen in the very near future, and thus focused their energies on being ready for the judgement and overthrow of all human authority, envisaged in the book of Revelation with great drama. In the meantime, Paul had told them, somewhat confusingly, to be obedient to governments as instituted by God. As the Church grew, the successive persecutions by the Roman emperors defined the place of Christians as those on the margins of acceptability in society.

All that began to change with the rule of Constantine, who was proclaimed emperor in York in 306. He slowly began his task of unifying a divided empire, by force when necessary, and achieved undisputed rule in 324. His adoption of the Christian faith was said to have dated from a mystical experience just before a critical battle in 312, and from hearing a direct call from God to fight under the sign of the cross. In fact, the nature and extent of Constantine's own faith is unclear; but, by the end of his life, Christianity had lost its pariah status and was beginning to enjoy privileges and rights which ensured its eventual place, after Constantine's death, as the official religion of the empire. Constantine, seeking further to impose unity through uniformity on his territories, also embroiled himself in Church debates on theology, calling and presiding over councils and synods, most famously the Council of Nicaea in 325 which defined the nature of Christ as both God and man. Constantine's gifts as a theologian were actually rather questionable; his self-confidence was certainly not. Having given Christianity such an extraordinary promotion, he had himself buried in Constantinople as Christ's thirteenth apostle.

Constantine is still central to Christian history because he set in motion a process which resulted in the integration of Church and State, and which continues to raise huge questions about the cost to integrity and truth when a religion allows itself to become a full partner in government. When the United States of America was eventually established in 1776, the founders and framers of the Constitution took the deliberate step of distancing themselves from such a possibility in their new country. They did so, not just against the background of their experience of the Church of England, whose Supreme Governor is the monarch, and whose bishops, appointed by the government, sit in the House of Lords, but also as a bold repudiation of the preceding two centuries, in which protracted and bloody wars had been fought over the religious division of Europe. The provision of the First Amendment to that constitution, which forbade the establishment of religion in the USA, was also a marked rejection of the country's own colonial past, in which the creation of areas of doctrinal and spiritual purity for certain denominations had been a central aim.

Christianity has thus profoundly shaped Western society in particular, because of this awkward marriage of spiritual and temporal authority. It is sometimes too easy to overlook the ways in which this may have been of benefit, for example, in the creation of some sense of national unity, in the inspiration of architecture, art and literature, and in the establishment of a moral or ethical framework. Very quickly after the beginning of this process, however, the Church was called upon to add theological weight to pressing affairs of state. None was more pressing than the need to have backing for the declaration of war, and thus Christian thinkers and writers from the time of Constantine onwards soon devoted their efforts and energies to that subject. If the very attempt to do so seems a far cry from the apparently pacifist and non-violent convictions of Jesus, it is a clear sign of how quickly Christianity's increased prestige was to come at a cost: as some would say, that of its own soul.

The Crusades, of course, represent the longest and worst episode in Christian violence and murderous intolerance. Their consequences are still being worked out: one compelling reason why modern Christians should know something about them. Pope Urban II declared the First Crusade in 1095, and it is estimated that up to 127,000 people responded to his call to take up arms in order to free Jerusalem from Muslim control. They did so even at personal cost, because of the new and striking way in which the Pope framed his summons. The Crusaders were assured that, in this act of obedience and adventure, they were benefitting their souls in a number of interrelated ways. First, the Crusade was defined as an act of penance, for which forgiveness for sins could be obtained. Second, it was a holy pilgrimage, to the holiest of cities, and thus profitable to those taking part. Finally, of course, it was called an act of obedience to Christ himself, through his representative the Pope, by which heretical infidels would be driven back and their murderous intentions to wipe the Christian faith from the earth thwarted. This theological definition was a work of genius, in the way that it stirred the hearts of so many Europeans to join the effort. One contemporary historian summarized its appeal:

> God has instituted in our time holy wars, so that the order of knights and the crowd running in their wake ... might find a new way of gaining salvation. And so they are not forced to abandon secular affairs completely by choosing the monastic life or any religious profession, as used to be the custom, but can attain in some measure God's grace while pursuing their own careers, with the liberty and in the dress to which they are accustomed.[1]

Equally, of course, it stirred anti-Muslim hatred, and also anti-Jewish sentiment. The Crusaders began a systematic campaign of violence against the Jews as they made their way east, which has left a similar scar on the modern world.

Although the crusade was a novel fusion of concepts and ideas, the theologians who joined them together were of course drawing on the work of earlier writers. Most notably, Augustine of Hippo had written about the circumstances under which, in his view, Christians could legitimately take up arms. He had taught that any war which involved Christians had to be waged for the common good, as defined by the monarch, had to have as its aim a 'just' cause, especially the punishing of evil, and had to be entered into with right intention. Hatred towards the opponent, bullying and gratuitous persecution of the conquered were strictly forbidden. Augustine allowed for Christian violence only when the sole aim was to secure an otherwise elusive peace. His ideas have been influential, and the first advocates of the Crusade drew on them extensively, arguing that the retaking of Jerusalem constituted the most just of causes and the highest defence of Christ himself. In other respects, however, their use of Augustine lacked the kind of hermeneutical rigour for which we might hope. He wrote his words after the fall of Rome in 410, against the background of an insecure and frightening world in which Christianity was often forced into a defensive position against pagan incursions. It is unlikely that Augustine would have equated his sense of a collapsing Christian world with the eleventh-century papacy's power, influence and control. The callous behaviour of the Crusaders, in any case, went well beyond the guidelines he sought to draw.

The Crusades had a long shelf-life, and in fact the concept of this kind of holy war was not formally rejected by the Church until the eighteenth century. In between, there were six 'official' Crusades, plus various 'People's Crusades', a Crusade involving children in 1212, which met with predictable disaster and carnage, and a Crusade launched by King Louis IX of France in 1248 whose glorious outcome was the capture of the King himself. His loyal subjects ransomed him. Crusades were also increasingly waged against groups of heretics in Europe, as a means to try and channel their popular appeal into other goals. In all of this, successive holders of the papacy stoked the fires, both of anti-Muslim and anti-Jewish feeling, and encouraged the establishment of communities of knights, or religious fighting orders, devoted solely to the aims and intentions of the Crusades. Some of them, such as the Knights Hospitallers of St John, survive to the present day, though with vastly different objectives. The Crusades remain a great scar on the soul of the Church, stretching through the medieval period and still affecting Christian relationships with the Muslim and Jewish faiths and those who practise them.

Heretics, too, were frequently subjected to gruesome and brutal punishments by the Church's authorities. Their stories further seem to cry out against the Church's past. Initially, those who professed beliefs at odds with what the Church, in council or by the determination of its leaders, declared and decided to be orthodox, were simply excluded from the common life of faith. Even Paul's letters envisage such a punishment for stubbornly independent thinkers. By the medieval period, similar factors to those which drove the Church authorities to proclaim Crusades led also to firmer treatment of heretics. The dreaded Spanish Inquisition, in fact, had as its prime founding cause in the fifteenth century the need to ensure that Jews converted – often forcibly – to Christianity did not bring any Jewish ideas with them. Only later did it become infamous as a body of torturers responsible for ensuring that all Catholics believed as they should. The whole Reformation period is littered with examples of horrible cruelty, across the board: Protestants burned by Queen Mary I of England; Catholic priests and their sympathizers hanged, drawn and quartered by Elizabeth I; a notorious heretic publicly executed by Calvin in Geneva; the massacre of tens of thousands of French Protestants on 24 August 1572, which one Catholic correspondent described as an event which 'not only delights the Christian world with admiration, but brings it to a peak of rejoicing'.[2] Is there any value to remembering such shameful episodes?

Saints or sinners?

How are we, centuries later, to receive this kind of troubling legacy and acknowledge it as anything belonging to us? One compelling figure from the Reformation period perhaps helps us to begin to reflect on these issues, by embodying the tension they create. Sir Thomas More, regarded as a saint in the Roman Catholic Church, remains one of the most fascinating, attractive and complex men of the sixteenth century. He rose to be Lord Chancellor of England under Henry VIII, and was the first layman to hold the office. More was widely praised even in his own day as a scholar, lawyer and statesman. His wit was legendary; his daughters benefitted from More's view, way ahead of its time, that women deserved an education too; his writings were lucid and persuasive, full of colour and intuitive insight into human nature. He was friends with the leading scholars of his day, and held his own with them, an ardent patron of the 'new learning', humanism, which was revolutionizing faith and thought across Europe. More's great personal crisis was that he correctly foresaw the inevitable consequence of the king's proposed divorce from Catherine of Aragon: the division of the European Church. He thus stood firmly in opposition to it, even at the cost of his career, his wealth, his health and ultimately his life. In facing a certain death, and in navigating the path from life as the King's friend and chief counsellor to death as a traitor, More's luminous faith, extraordinary courage and unfailing charm never faltered. He was truly a 'man for all seasons', who continues to beguile and inspire people of all faiths and none.

Those who discover the fullness of More's convictions and actions are often shocked. For he was a fierce prosecutor – some would say persecutor – of heresy and of heretics. His literary talents were also turned against Martin Luther, in language that was certainly unfit for those of a nervous disposition (Luther responded in kind). When Lutheran preachers and disseminators were found in England, More boasted a career in hunting them down that few could rival. He favoured their imprisonment and encouraged that those who refused to repent or who later relapsed into heretical thinking be burned alive. Lutherans, such as Simon Bilney and John Frith, who attempted to bring the new religion across the English Channel, found in Thomas More an implacable opponent who saw in their death a foretaste of the fires of hell which awaited them. Is More really the man we thought he was?

The difficulty many feel about this apparent conflict in More's character lies in a failure to understand his context, a failure which comes back to the kind of methodology we discussed in Chapter 3. It is illustrative of the whole dilemma we have outlined here. More's persecuting tendencies were most famously, and dramatically, described by John Foxe a generation later. As we have seen, Foxe's *Book of Martyrs* was written as a review of the shameful and violent treatment of 'Protestants' throughout the Church's history. More's notoriety was ensured by Foxe's colourful descriptions of his bloodlust, which were often wildly exaggerated. Not only that, but Foxe demonstrates again how history is written by the winners, and how their perspective shapes the attitudes of a whole society:

Catholicism was formally and legally tolerated in England only in 1829, and remained an object of deep suspicion and mistrust even after that. More is thus fixed as a Catholic, a persecutor and a murderer – that was Foxe's intention. In fact, More's views on heresy were universally held in his day. It was, in a Catholic Christendom, viewed in similar terms to the plague: a dangerous infection which, if left unchecked, threatened not just the Church or individual faith, but the whole fabric of the nation and the safety of the country. Heretics undermined societal cohesion and were the enemies of peace and good order. They were traitors of the vilest kind. More, along with everyone else, thought that losing a heretic was better than national anarchy and ruin. Nor were John Foxe's own views much different: he just thought that it was Catholics who deserved to suffer violence.

Such an understanding does not excuse or validate violence; but it does demand that we not expect from people from the distant past decisions that, in their context and culture, they simply could not have made. It's a distinction, though, that needs to be handled very carefully. There may be a difference between accepting an inherited worldview and fearing the consequences of great religious change, like Thomas More, and devising a whole new category of and model for violent, hateful conduct, like Pope Urban II. In making this kind of judgement, it is also vital to be attentive to the surrounding voices of the time, and to feel for the limits of what was then possible. The early Church father, Gregory of Nazianzus, came to the view in the fourth century that the institution of slavery was wicked and sinful, and that it was a vile thing for one human being to possess another. He was a lone voice. Indeed, it took another fifteen centuries for his view to prevail: and we are forced to ask whether others could have, and should have, reached the same conclusion earlier. Similarly, those who use this argument to defend those Church leaders in Germany in the 1930s who failed to grasp the evil of Nazi ideology are on thin ice: plenty of others managed it.

Such distinctions are necessary, but not really helpful to the wider point. How are modern Christians to view this sorry aspect of their past? What sense, use or purpose is there in such a shameful catalogue of injustice, warfare and cruelty? To revert to the imagery we used earlier: do we really have to retain our bad memories too? If it is a mistake, either to forget such formative but horrible events, or to attempt simply to start our faith again on a blank sheet, how shall we ever come to terms, usefully, repentantly and creatively, with these things? As a beginning, we should contemplate three perspectives.

First, we need the memory of these periods of our history *as a means to enabling a contemporary conversation*. The way in and extent to which the Church should be involved with government and the machinery of the State remains a vital question. As Christians and their spiritual leaders aspire to 'speak truth to power', from what position can that best be done? History offers a number of models, from Constantinian unity between religion and politics to the ideal (not in fact entirely realized) of American separation. The Church of England, true to its nature, finds itself still navigating a middle way, with significant access to national leaders and a residual role in government and the State, but without real political power. Still, in countries where the Church is intimately bound up with government as in those where it belongs to the margins of society, the questions are compelling and urgent, and it is folly to overlook the ways in which they have worked out elsewhere and earlier. To make a slogan of the dilemma, should we be independent but impotent, or influential but inauthentic? Christians who find it easy to judge the past are often being less than open about the ways in which these discussions are still continuing. They are also refusing to be honest about how these questions still divide and affect Christians, who can hardly be said to be of one mind.

The issue of whether and in what circumstances Christians should ever condone or take part in war is similarly far from settled: would that it were. Some think that the religion of Jesus of Nazareth can only be a pacifist religion, whose aderents should refuse to go to war under any circumstances. Others sense that some causes are still 'just' and deserving of military intervention: the need to end the Nazi regime and the perpetration of the Shoah would be one example. Some – former President George W. Bush, for example – would still talk of some of these enterprises, like the second Iraq War and the ousting of the extremist Muslim Taliban regime in Afghanistan, in terms of a 'crusade'. In any case, every major world power keeps an army and devotes resources to its maintenance. Should the Church still be supplying these armed forces with chaplaincy support, and, if so, on what grounds and for what purpose? If the Christian Church is to have an informed, measured and profitable discussion about these concepts and their ethical value, a knowledge of how the conversation has previously been conducted, and how the conclusions of the argument fell out when implemented, is essential. Here we clearly glimpse again the need to marry those twin historical sciences; we must compare the way in which Augustine's thinking about 'just war' has come down to us through the evolution of time and circumstance with our own sense of how it might directly 'project' from then to now, from one world to another. We are at liberty, after all, either to conclude that it is no longer needed or radically to redefine its terms.

Even beyond the obvious point that there is still a debate in the twenty-first-century Church about war and peace, which needs to be informed and have a historical perspective, there is a wider question which ought to undermine the smugness of those who easily and breezily dismiss so much of the past through a misguided sense of human 'progress'. It concerns the continued prevalence of what we might term 'spiritual violence', the ongoing attempt within many sections of the Church to diminish or exclude others on theological grounds because of their difference. This can happen because of race, gender, sexual identity, theological outlook or socio-economic factors. Those Christians who indulge in it need to be able to explain

how their mindset and actions differ from previous generations who persecuted Jews, despised 'infidels' or marginalized
those thought inferior because of birth, background or belief.
If progress through history has been so clear and unambiguous,
why do such prejudices remain? And how are we ever to dis-
cuss their validity and character, if we have no reference points
against which to compare them? The debate about Christianity
and the State, war and violence is as current as ever – and is
severely impoverished if Christians lose their memory.

Second, it is only through retaining the memory of these kinds
of issues that we *honour the victims of violence and identify its
causes and its authors*. In a sermon entitled 'Remembering for
the Future', Archbishop Rowan Williams stressed the importance of these two duties, quoting Eliot's description of history
as something which may liberate or enslave us.[3] At a basic
level, we might recall the old saying that to forget the past is to
be doomed to repeat it. There is certainly truth in that: Christians in each succeeding generation will need to reflect on how
their ancestors gave in to political pressure, or the influence of
power, at the cost of their religious integrity. Such temptations
are always present but often hard to recognize. Understanding
that we are as liable to compromise our basic beliefs, albeit in
different ways, as our distant cousins in faith, we read their history with hearts more broken by their cruelty and more aware
of our own conflictedness and guilt. We also take seriously the
memory and human dignity of those who suffered their violence. The story of Christian violence demonstrates again and
again that the truly great figures of faith are those able to rise
above the prevailing thought patterns of their age and recall
believers to a more genuine and authentic practice of belief. It
is for their sake too that we must not forget.

This particular duty has been given sharp and painful focus
by the Shoah. Hitler's genocide of six million Jews, not to
mention other excluded social groups, has forced the Christian Church into an agonizing realization of how hateful its
own history and teaching have been. Centuries of anti-Jewish

theology and practice in the Church laid the foundation for Nazi thought and offered the regime the resources to frame and implement its horrifying measures. No modern Christian should be unaware of this.[4] And only the retention of our collective memory enables us, both to honour those who perished and to recognize our own part, as Western Christians, in their murder. Susan White suggests that, alongside the difficult question, 'Where was God at Auschwitz?', we should ask another: 'Where was I?'. For the most part, we would find ourselves, not among the lines of people outside the gas chambers, but among the silent, unprotesting lines of worshippers, sat in pews every Sunday, members of a church whose teaching about the Jews over centuries was contributing to the deaths of our sisters and brothers in faith. The Jewish theologian Emil Fackenheim suggested an addition to the Torah, a '614th Commandment', whose principle was simple: allow Hitler no posthumous victories.[5] Ignorance of this aspect of our history, silence about our complicity and the failure of the Church, or a refusal to acknowledge our corporate memory and guilt, would certainly violate it.

Finally, and more hopefully, cherishing even the difficult and painful parts of our history also reveals to us *that a penitent tradition has the creative ability to renew itself*. The appalling way in which the Church condoned slavery and the brutalization of Africans for centuries was eventually overthrown late in the eighteenth century by a sea-change in thought and theology. The resources for this, however, were already within the tradition, and not simply dreamed up in the minds of a few philanthropists. The unprecented horrors of the Shoah have begun to produce serious renewal in Christian theology and liturgy, in ways that recognize that the Jews are still God's precious covenant people, and which have removed from the language of public worship much of the vitriol and condemnation of earlier years. Again, this work cannot simply ignore the past; it must go back further and down deeper, to find authentic resources with which to reject old perversions of the faith and fashion a new response. There is still a long way to go: but, against the record of human tribalism, prejudice and intolerance, in which for too long the Church has been a willing partner, we might place the openheartedness of the mystical tradition, George Herbert's gentle evocation of divine grace, the 'Catholic Spirit' of John Wesley, the extraordinary dignity of the Quakers, or the twentieth-century rejuvenation of the power of non-violent protest by Mahatma Gandhi and Martin Luther King. Given that we cannot be selective in our remembering, to be altogether forgetful requires us also to reject such remarkable and vital teachers and guides as these. So, let us go deeper here, and spend a while recognizing just how deeply some causes and ideas which we count as 'modern' run in the Christian tradition. They are one counterpoint to the tragedies we have examined, and demonstrate how timeless and tireless is the fight for justice, begun by Jesus himself on the foundation of the prophets who came before him. That fight continues – sometimes addressed to the internal faults of the Church, but more often toward the transformation of the world.

Freeing the poor, saving the planet: new wine from old wineskins

The twentieth century witnessed change and technological progress at an unprecedented and extraordinary rate. Those born in the early part of the century would hardly recognize the place the world had become by the end of their lives. Caught up in this whirlwind of scientific, cultural and intellectual advance, it was tempting for citizens of that century to assume that they were entering uncharted territory, drawing the maps for themselves, throwing off the shackles of the past and beginning a new phase of human achievement and glory. The 'postmodern' system of thought and action was founded on this way of regarding the new world order. And yet, the last century also brought with it parallel developments in warfare and weaponry which wiped out whole generations and races, an all-powerful system of market economics which simply swallowed up those too weak or poor to compete and survive, and an increasingly globalized world which, for all its benefits, served also to make wider and deeper the chasm between the world's richest and poorest nations. In its quest to evangelize the world, the Church and its missionaries have been a key factor in this process, often confusing their religious message with the Western culture in which, for them, it was embedded.

At the beginning of the twenty-first century, one of the most serious results of the operation of the global markets and the raping of the earth for resources is the immediate threat of an environmental catastrophe of unprecedented magnitude. Human consumption and demand for mobility and energy have led to the poisoning of the atmosphere and the endangering of the very planet itself. The Intergovernmental Panel on Climate Change (IPCC), made up of hundreds of scientists from across the globe, has in recent years produced a series of reports, whose precise scholarly language does not disguise the urgency and force of their message. In summary, the IPCC states: that carbon dioxide is increasing in the earth's atmosphere; that, consequently, the planet is slowly warming; and that, beyond all reasonable doubt, human activity is to blame. The medium-term results of this, as icecaps melt and sea levels rise, will be nothing short of devastating. In Africa, the area from Senegal to Somalia has already witnessed the worst floods in 50 years. Parts of Kenya face a 25 per cent *decrease* in annual rainfall. In all, 250 million African people will face severe water shortages, and the yield from rain-fed crops may be halved by 2020. In Bangladesh, the rising oceans will cover up to 20 per cent of the country, causing hunger, disease, mass migration and competition for scarce natural resources. Overall, one billion Asians will be affected by these processes. Parts of the former Soviet Union, too, are already experiencing extreme drought. Even as brief a survey as this makes another point very forcibly: climate change most affects the poorest parts of the world. The developing world will bear the brunt of the unchecked consumption and unmitigated greed of the West.

As this monumental crisis has developed and loomed, the Christian Church has been rather mixed in its response. Indeed, there has even been a debate about whether to respond at all. For some, the issue was a distraction from the real business of saving souls. Such people generally took the view that, since the world was going to end at some point anyway – when Jesus returned – there was no real reason for concern. The global environment was an expendable resource, a temporary earthly dwelling-place which merely prepared us for heaven. The strident reaction of the religious right in the USA encapsulated this point of view. The late Jerry Falwell, founder of Liberty University and the 'Moral Majority' movement, described the question of whether and how to respond to climate change as 'Satan's attempt to re-direct the Church's primary focus'. His colleague, Ted Haggard, said while President of the National Association of Evangelicals that it was 'not a consensus issue' and therefore of low priority. Ironically, he, like Falwell, preferred to concentrate on issues like abortion and same-sex relationships; the latter soon proved his own undoing and formed another consensus: that he should resign. Others railed against the 'junk science' of the IPCC, which they claimed was luring Christians towards paganism. These prominent Christians all made their case on the basis that working to save the planet was somehow not a Christian cause, and an act of infidelity to the gospel, if chosen above converting sinners and preaching hell-fire.

They were wrong. As other Christians began to seek for theological tools to help them address the ecological emergency, they discovered a rich heritage on which to draw. Centrally, the investigation revealed how much the modern Christian emphasis on individual, personal salvation was a recent invention. Previous generations, by contrast, had taken a far less narrow, and far more inclusive, view. Instead of concentrating only on 'me and my soul', the Christian faith actually contained beautiful and compelling testimonies to a God-given sense of oneness with all creation, and of how all creation, together with humanity, was within the scope of Christ's saving work. From Genesis 2, in which humans are seen, not as the peak and pinnacle of God's creative work, but rather in the midst of it, to Jesus asking his listeners to consider lilies and birds if they wanted to know about God's care of creation, and way beyond, a very different perspective was on offer. And, while the need to proclaim the good news of grace, forgiveness and the renewal of human community was still great, the seeds of an authentically Christian voice on the climate crisis lay in these ways of thinking, acting and praying.

The first Christian hermits we met in the previous chapter were in some sense the pioneers of this closeness with nature in the early Church. Alone in the desert with only their prayers, stories soon grew up of their friendships with wild animals and their growing harmony with the earth of which they increasingly felt a part. Many adopted a vegetarian diet; some were said to have been fed, and even clothed, by desert creatures. One, Macarius the Alexandrian, it was claimed, had been suckled by a sympathetic and accommodating buffalo in a moment of extreme hunger. However fantastic such tales seem to us, they reflect the ways in which these early spiritual giants viewed themselves as part of the good earth which held them and all creatures in its embrace.

These Desert Mothers and Fathers also bequeathed a strong sense of nature's wonder and integrity to their monastic descendants, the Celtic Christians of the early medieval period. The latter lived out their lives and exercised their evangelistic vocation amid the spectacular scenery of Ireland, Scotland, Wales and northern England. In all their writings, and in their liturgy, their sense of their oneness with creation is constantly and powerfully described. St Columba of Iona in the sixth century sought to deepen this connection by standing in the sea, up to his neck, for overnight prayer vigils. He and his contemporaries emphasized the sacramental quality of the earth: that it was in the material beauty of the created order that God's constant presence was constantly to be found by the prayerful. Work and worship, life and death, heaven and earth were one uninterrupted cycle of God's goodness and love, theatres for God's gracious acts, and witnesses to God's closeness. A century before Columba, St Patrick had revealed the same theology – and love of creation – in his famous 'Breastplate':

I bind unto myself this day
The virtues of the star-lit heaven,
The glorious sun's life-giving ray,
The whiteness of the moon at even,
The flashing of the lightning free,
The whirling wind's tempestuous shocks,
The stable earth, the deep salt sea
Around the old eternal rocks.[6]

The medieval mystical writers and thinkers carried forward and developed this Christian concern for and connection with the earth. In particular, though not exclusively, it was women mystics who devoted prayerful attention to this area. Perhaps the most remarkable of them all was the 'Renaissance Woman', Hildegard of Bingen (1098–1179), a German nun, scholar, artist, playwright, scientist and composer who held the great distinction in her day of being the only woman itinerant preacher of the entire medieval period. Hildegard was a leader in the development of the monastic movement, founding several new convents within her Benedictine order. Her scientific writing included learned and careful treatises on natural history and the form and design of animals, as well as on minerals, rocks and flora. In all of this, her acute theological mind saw a deeper connection between humanity and the world it inhabits. From the earth and its fertility, she reminded her readers, human beings themselves are created and nourished, including the man at the centre of Christian faith and life:

The earth of humankind contains all moistness,
all verdancy,
all germinating power.
It is in so many ways fruitful,
All creation comes from it,
yet it forms not only the basic raw material for humankind
but also the substance of the incarnation of God's Son.

Moving beyond patriarchal ideas of 'dominion' over the earth, Hildegard emphasized its God-given 'viriditas', or 'green power', a selfless energy offered freely to and shared by all life.[7]
Later mystics continued to develop Hildegard's perception that she was enfolded with *all* creation in the care of a loving Creator. Francis of Assisi in the twelfth century famously called the sun his brother and the moon his sister, and wrote a hymn which summoned the whole cosmos to a great song of united praise. A generation after him, the German mystic Meister Eckhart expanded further on Hildegard's theology, and became an advocate for the use of feminine imagery for God: appropriate, he thought, because of God's abundant fertility as Creator. The hand of that creating God could still be seen, he believed, in every single thing made, and in this humans had no special advantage or grace. 'If I spent enough time with the tiniest creature – even a caterpillar,' he reflected, 'I would never have to prepare a sermon. So full of God is every creature.' His insight was most famously mirrored in the writings of the English mystic Julian of Norwich (1342–1413), who claimed that 'the day of my spiritual awakening was the day I saw, and knew I saw, God in all things and all things in God'. Julian's deep confidence that 'all shall be well' was rooted in her apprehension of God's loving concern for 'everything that is made', a reassurance most strikingly glimpsed in her vision of the whole created order, held in the palm of God's hand as though it were a hazelnut.[8]
Later generations of Christian leaders and writers, too, demonstrate how recent – and how false – is the modern obsession

with self at the expense of the world around us. In the seventeenth century in England, the Anglican Thomas Traherne wrote of his respect for the face of the world around him, and his humility when enjoying it, in language that is reminiscent of Julian:

> You never enjoy the world aright, till you see how a [grain of] sand exhibiteth the wisdom and power of God: and prize in everything the service which they can do to you, by manifesting his glory and goodness to your Soul ... Yet further, you never enjoy the world aright, till you so love the beauty of enjoying it, that you are covetous and earnest to persuade others to enjoy it. And so perfectly hate the abominable corruption of men in despising it, that you had rather suffer the flames of Hell than willingly be guilty of their error.[9]

Traherne reads like the patron saint of the environmental movement. His evocations of the wonder of children, delighting in nature and making dazzling new discoveries daily, and his call to adults to reclaim this awe, are some of the most remarkable passages of nature writing in English literature. His essential reverence for nature – not as divine, but as invested with divine presence and love – was reflected in subsequent Christian movements. The Quakers and their founder George Fox are one example, as is the eighteenth-century founder of Methodism, John Wesley, who was characteristically optimistic that the plan of salvation did not end with humanity. 'The whole creation', he declared, 'will undoubtedly be restored ... with beauty, happiness will return.'[10]

It is worth taking some time to become acquainted with voices like these. They speak, throughout history, of the way in which, as Gerard Manley Hopkins wrote, 'the world is charged with the grandeur of God'.[11] They offered a deep, rich seam of insight for modern theologians such as Jürgen Moltmann, Rubem Alves and Douglas John Hall, as they formulated their 'ecotheology', partly as a response to the witness of the environmental movement. They also offer a corrective to the excessively individualized approach to faith and theology which became predominant in the West as technology advanced, the markets boomed and personal gain became the goal of every human life. Christians can find authority in their faith's heritage for a passionate, dedicated response to the abuse and destruction of the planet; they do not by doing so neglect the gospel, but rather live it out. The earth is a partner with us in creation, and a partner with us in salvation. By fighting for the proper care of the environment too, Christians are working with and alongside the poorest peoples of the world. In that struggle, too, an extraordinary renewal in recent decades has reflected deep concerns and insights from the past.

Theologies of liberation

When Bishop Gerardi of Guatemala stood in solidarity with his people, demanding systemic change to protect them from corruption and allow them to live in freedom and peace, he was reflecting the principles of a remarkable movement of 'bottom-up' theology that swept Central and South America in the second half of the twentieth century. Liberation Theology, as it became known, arose from a grass-roots revolution. Small groups of local Christians, known technically as base ecclesial communities, began to reflect together on the systems which confined their flourishing as human beings: a colonial past; the imposition of a foreign faith and belief system; grinding poverty caused and made worse by successive governments; a complete marginalization in the life of their nations. Their work of faith led in time to a corresponding call for change from some Church leaders and theologians. Theology, they said, should no longer be 'done to' the people. It should begin from where they are. It should address their concerns and speak to their needs and aspirations. And it should be enacted, in ways that free God's children from violence, want and fear, in ways that oppose repression and build up justice. In the words of Leonardo Boff, one of the movement's leading theologians:

> The theology of liberation seeks to establish that the kingdom of God is to be established not only in the *soul* ... and not only in *heaven* ... but in relationships among human beings as well ... In sum, liberation theology is a theology that seeks to take history, and Christians' historical responsibility, seriously.[12]

Liberation Theology understands itself as inaugurating a new way of doing theology in relation to the State: neither simply protesting against, and certainly not conserving, the status quo, but rather building a new social order, based on theological values. In this self-understanding, many leading thinkers in the movement soon found themselves battling against Catholic bishops, both in Latin America and the Vatican. People like Boff, Jon Sobrino and Gustavo Gutiérrez were criticized for leading Christianity along a 'Marxist' path, rooted in a sense of 'class struggle' and crossing the line which forbad priests to be politically active. The accusation was aptly summarized by Helder Camara, a Brazilian archbishop and supporter of the movement's aims: 'When I give food to the poor,' he is said to have observed, 'they call me a saint. When I ask why the poor have no food, they call me a Communist'. Pope John Paul II, whose resistance of communism in his native Poland made him alert to these nuances and fiercely resistant to them, took action against some whose views he judged dangerous, even offering an extremely lukewarm tribute to Archbishop Romero; John Paul believed Romero's murder was the inevitable result of his political advocacy for the poor of El Salvador. In this attack, the Pope was ably and willingly supported by Cardinal Joseph Ratzinger, his theological enforcer and eventual successor. The conflict exposed the struggle between old and new (or, as the liberation theologians saw it, old and even older, and thus more authentic) understandings of faith, as the entrenched, hierarchical men in Rome tried to silence those seeking to make the Church more receptive to the needs of all its members: rich and poor, male and female, black and white, powerful and powerless.

Although Liberation theologians at first saw themselves as doing a new thing, they have lately begun to acknowledge the roots their movement has in the past, from the Hebrew prophets and their constant cries for justice, onward. To mention just a few: Boff himself spoke of the debt his thinking owed to St Francis, who in the thirteenth century came to understand his calling as complete identification with Christ through complete identification with the poor. Provision for the local poor, indeed, was a central vocation of the whole medieval monastic movement. Two centuries after Francis, Nicolas Rolin and his wife, Guigone de Salins, were inspired by their faith to devote a great portion of their wealth to the construction of a grand refuge for the poor, who had been made increasingly destitute by long wars and were under constant threat of disease and death. The complex of buildings they built in Beaune, France, remains one of the most outstanding pieces of architecture from the time, and exemplifies how lavish their hospitality was towards the lowest and least. They stand also as an eloquent counterpoint to the Church's involvement in the wars which led to their construction. Gerard Winstanley in the sixteenth century even foreshadowed Liberation Theology's methods and consequences, by insisting that 'tradesmen will speak by experience the things they have seen in God, and the learned clergy will be slighted'.[13] 'True godliness', the Quaker William Penn urged in 1682, 'does not turn people out of the world, but enables them to live better in it and excites their endeavours to mend it.'[14] Through the ages, many Christians have quietly built upon Jesus' declaration that the poor uniquely possess God's blessing.

By seeking not just charity but justice, and a material change in the structures which cause poverty, others have reflected Penn's optimism and in some way foreshadowed Liberation

Theology. The most effective were those who emerged from the eighteenth-century Enlightenment. The Methodist movement, for example, was profoundly shaped by John Wesley's growing passion for the poor. He despised the British aristocracy, and found his place ever more with those beyond the boundaries of respectable society. From his days as a student in Oxford, he had seen the creation of wealth as a benefit only if it allowed those with money to alleviate the condition of the poor. He encouraged the Methodists not to become too rich, and to live on an absolute minimum budget in order to maximize their giving; he often expressed his doubts and distrust concerning investments and wealth speculation. Wesley also understood the need not simply to give money, and his movement offered health care, shelter and, most important of all, education to those who lacked them. He exerted some influence in his day in advocating for social reform; certainly, he saw continued poverty as an outrageous injustice perpetrated by the rich. All this was founded on a theology which, against the thinking of the day, insisted that poverty was not a punishment from God, because God desired all people alike to know the love and grace revealed in Jesus.[15]

Wesley's most colourful descendant was arguably General William Booth, whose 'Salvation Army' sought to cherish this Methodist bias to the poor. Indeed, the General claimed – in front of the Methodist Conference, in fact, with admirable chutzpah – that the Army had 'gone on, only a great deal further, on the lines he travelled'. Booth and his wife Catherine tirelessly fought against poverty and its consequences, including addiction, prostitution and high child mortality rates. After his wife's death, Booth's great work, *In Darkest England, and the Way Out*, described the scandal of English poverty and offered radical measures for its eradication. The summary of a recent biographer reveals how Booth's work was both linked to the Christian past and strikingly similar, almost a century before its emergence, to the methods of Liberation Theology:

St. Francis was cited in support of the Salvation Army's operating methods – the personal association of the Army with the families which it aimed to help. 'Slum sisters' lived amongst, and in barely better conditions than, the men and women they hoped to save from degradation. As a result, they could speak on the subject with the authority which came from real experience.[16]

Booth's army, of course, continues his work and cherishes his legacy, to this day, and across the globe.

That the Church has such a noble tradition of following the biblical call to care for the earth and work alongside the poor is no claim that its involvement in and perpetration of violence can be ignored or excused. By tracing it, though, we do begin to discover something of that rich harmony of voices which make up the history of the Church's interaction with the world. Succeeding generations have interpreted and used Jesus Christ in ways quite different from one another, for good and for ill, and influenced, variously, by the needs, mindset and wickedness of the age. At the very least, we should learn from that process of interaction something about the ways in which we too unthinkingly enlist God to our side or assume that Jesus himself would endorse our cause. In this history, both heartening and dispiriting, inspiring and appalling, we glimpse the possibilities of our human nature, which can use anything, even religion, to increase and secure its own power, but which faith, uniquely, can also raise to heights of unimaginable passion and purpose.

The sick, entering the Hôtel Dieu in Beaune, were led from the filth and squalor of their existence to the infirmary, where they were laid in a cushioned four-poster bed and nursed until they recovered – or died. As they entered, they saw a statue of Christ, sat on a stone at Calvary, his head crowned with thorns, bound hand and foot, his body marred and bruised from torture and beating. He is waiting to be nailed to his cross. In his total desolation, his identification with the frail scraps of humanity who passed by must have seemed complete. Five hundred years after the building of the Hôtel Dieu, amid the squalor and depravity of a war which destroyed a whole generation, the poet Wilfred Owen came across a wayside crucifix in the French countryside. He was overcome by the same paradox: his own identification with this broken, dying man, and the hope of the nobler life to which he still calls humanity, even as those who claim to follow him send others to a brutal death:

> One ever hangs where shelled roads part.
> In this war he too lost a limb,
> But his disciples hide apart;
> And now the soldiers bear with him.

> Near Golgotha strolls many a priest,
> And in their faces there is pride
> That they were flesh-marked by the Beast
> By whom the gentle Christ's denied.

> The scribes on all the people shove
> And bawl allegiance to the state,
> But they who love the greater love
> Lay down their life; they do not hate.[17]

Notes

1 Guibert of Nogent, quoted by Jonathan Riley-Smith, in *The Crusades: A History*, New Haven and London: Yale University Press, 2005, p. 14.

2 Letter of Joachim Opser, quoted in Joel Harrington (ed.), *A Cloud of Witnesses*, Boston: Houghton Mifflin, 2001, p. 281.

3 Rowan Williams, *Open to Judgement: Sermons and Addresses*, London: Darton Longman and Todd, 1994, pp. 237–42.

4 Any who are should read, for example, Jocelyn Hellig's excellent *The Holocaust and Antisemitism*, Oxford: Oneworld, 2003, or Steven Smith, Carol Rittner and Irena Steinfeld, *The Holocaust and the Christian World*, London: Kuperard, 2000.

5 Emil Fackenheim, *God's Presence in History*, New York: New York University Press, 1970, pp. 67–98, and *To Mend the World*, Bloomington and Indianapolis: Indiana University Press, 1970, pp. xixff.

6 This famous hymn may not be by Patrick, though it is attributed to him. In any case, it reflects authentically the Celtic worldview.

7 Dorothy Soelle's classic *The Silent Cry*, Minneapolis: Fortress Press, 2001, remains one of the best introductions to mysticism and includes a chapter on mystic meditation on nature.

8 Eckhart quotation (unreferenced) in *Iona Abbey Worship Book*, Glasgow: Wild Goose, 2001, p. 138; Mother Julian's first and third Revelations, quoted in Paul Handley et al. (eds), *The English Spirit*, London: Darton, Longman and Todd, 1987, p. 43.

9 Thomas Traherne, *Centuries*, London: Faith Press, 1960, pp. 13–15.

10 Sermon LXV on The General Deliverance, in *Sermons on Several Occasions* (Vol. II), London: J. Kershaw, 1825, pp. 121–32.

11 In his poem, 'God's Grandeur'.

12 From *Liberation Theology: From Confrontation to Dialogue* (1985), quoted in Harrington, *A Cloud of Witnesses*, p. 506.

13 Quoted by Christopher Rowland, in *The Cambridge Companion to Liberation Theology*, Cambridge: Cambridge University Press, 1999, p. 11.

14 Quoted in Catherine Whitmire, *Plain Living: A Quaker Path to Simplicity*, Notre Dame: Sorin, 2001, p. 175.

15 Henry Rack, *Reasonable Enthusiast*, London: Epworth Press, 1989, pp. 360–70.

16 Roy Hattersley, *Blood and Fire*, London: Little, Brown, 1999, pp. 161 and 370.

17 'At a Calvary near the Ancre', in Wilfred Owen, *The Poems of Wilfred Owen*, ed. Jon Stallworthy, London: Chatto and Windus, 1990, p. 111.

6

THE WHOLE INHABITED
EARTH

Ecumenism and Dialogue

The Anglican Diocese of Leicester was, after a hiatus of a few
hundred years, refounded in 1935. To celebrate its fiftieth anni-
versary in 1985, the Archbishop of Canterbury, Dr Robert
Runcie, made a visit to the city. The local Hindus reached out
to him, offering an invitation to visit their temple as a ges-
ture of friendship and goodwill, and he agreed, thus becoming
the first in his position to do so. Neither the Hindus nor the
Anglicans, however, had much experience of dealing with each
other, and were nervous about ensuring the visit was a suc-
cess; and so they turned to their interreligious experts to find
speeches which would be gracious and meaningfully authentic:
and yet would not make any unfortunate gaffes. The Hindus
turned to the secretary of the local Council of Faiths, which
was not long formed. He was a Methodist minister, but had
a deep knowledge and understanding of other faith traditions
and had been something of a pioneer in Leicester's interreligious scene, so necessary there after the extraordinary increase
in ethnic diversity the city had seen since the 1960s. The Anglicans turned to someone known to the Archbishop's secretary
as a reliable and sensitive friend of other faith traditions, who
also had deep connections in Leicester. Ironically, it was the

same local Methodist minister. He describes how, on the day of the visit, he sat in the temple and listened to two speeches, one given by the president of the temple, the other by the Primate of All England: both of which he had written.[1]

Only in recent decades has a story like this become even remotely possible. The shrinking of the world by the process of globalization, which we noted in the previous chapter, has also drawn together distant cultures and nations through migration and technological advance. One significant part of this change is the greater knowledge we now have of other living faith traditions; no longer are Muslims, Hindus or Sikhs distant people living halfway across the globe: they are our neighbours, those next to us at the supermarket checkout or in the doctors' surgery, the people who read our gas meter, teach our children, read the television news, represent us in Parliament and lead us in government. Even 50 years ago, such a situation would have been beyond reasonable belief or expectation. Along with this extraordinary reducing of the space between peoples and faiths has come a profound challenge for Western Christians: how to respond to this new and unprecedented diversity in our communities. While most reasonable, humane people have understood that the old medieval hatred and distrust for those who are not Christians won't do any longer, they have struggled often to know what model of engagement to use, to understand what the faith tradition in which they have been raised has to say about meeting with representatives of other religious traditions as neighbours and friends. Indeed, does it have anything to say? Or, is this an area in which Christians simply have to erase the memory of the past entirely and begin afresh, in order to be faithful to Christ in a world which neither he nor those who followed him for almost 2,000 years could have imagined?

The need to know how to engage with those of other religions has arisen alongside the movement to seek reconciliation with Christians of other denominations. Sometimes, the ecumenical movement, as it has become known, has been seen as the forerunner of the interreligious one, a sort of easy 'try out' for more complex conversations seeking a more elusive unity. In fact, the two have an interwoven history which dates back to the beginning of the twentieth century and even earlier. Their common origins lie in the eighteenth- and nineteenth-century missionary movements which, while they did much harm in assuming that Western culture should be imposed on foreign nations along with Western religion, also gave birth to some of the earliest practitioners of interreligious conversations, people whose purpose was more respectful and gracious than merely the intent to convert 'heathen'. We shall meet a few of them later. Second, the missionaries eventually came to realize that the divided and fragmented nature of their witness – Baptists evangelizing here, and Lutherans there, and the Methodists doing their own thing somewhere else – was a wasteful and needless handicap. Such was the tenor of the conversation, for example, at the World Missionary Conference held in Edinburgh in 1910, at which the Protestant churches declared their desire to foster a closer working relationship in order to maximize the effectiveness of their missions, and to understand the beliefs of others more respectfully in a missionary context. It was a move which perhaps did something to mitigate the legacy of so much of the missionary endeavour.

With the usual sloth of the Church, the World Council of Churches (WCC) came into being in 1948, a mirror in the Christian world to the establishing of the United Nations. The Roman Catholic Church withheld from membership until rather later, but the Protestant churches pursued the original insights of the missionaries, even in 1951 couching their understanding of their shared, 'ecumenical' mission in very similar terms. It was, they said, 'the whole task of the whole Church to bring the Gospel to the whole world'.[2] In their task of re-integration, however, the churches were faced with a similar struggle to find authority for their work. They looked to and were inspired by the words of Jesus in John's Gospel: 'that they may be one, as you and I are one',[3] and by what was seen as the scandal of division in the body of Christ. But it was hard to escape from the notion that, in fact, the ecumenical movement represented only an abandonment of the past, a complete rejection of centuries of Christian history in which the only movement had been toward fragmentation, and the splintering of Christ's people into smaller and smaller groups, each convinced to some degree that it alone possessed the truth. That view of the ecumenical vision, its sense of shame at Christian history and consequent rejection of it, is a common contemporary attitude. Though we need to be pentitent when neccesary, however, it is not the whole truth.

The very term which was used, from the nineteenth century onwards, to describe this effort is fascinating for what it reveals. The Greek word *oikumene*, from which the first pioneers of unity drew their title, is usually translated as 'the whole inhabited earth', and is a word generally used (at least in Greek) to describe everything that is, all that is made and all who live in it. It perhaps indicates the vestigial arrogance of Christians that this word should be used of the drive towards the healing of the Church's wounds. Christians can make no claim, except in a moment of theological imperialism, truly to represent 'the whole inhabited earth'. The interreligious movement has been called 'the new ecumenism', and perhaps has more claim to the word. In any case, the name stuck, and has persisted. Nowadays most Christians know what is meant by it, and that 'ecumenism' is only a means to the end of a united Christian mission and witness, and not an end in itself.

Before considering the ways in which ecumenism might find authority, precedent and guiding wisdom, even within the Church's sad history of fragmentation, we should consider the role of the Roman Catholic Church in the process. It has often brought to the table an understanding of the historical process, and of history, which has not helped to forge deeper unity. We met Pope Pius IX earlier, and his dramatic assertion, at the First Vatican Council of 1870, 'I *am* the tradition!'. His successor and namesake, Pius XI, affirmed a similar point of view in 1928 by describing the only acceptable form of ecumenism as being the wholesale return of the Orthodox and Protestant churches to Rome – a neat solution, sadly flawed by its lack of both realism and grace. The theological basis for this view, of course, is a particular notion of tradition itself, and the way in which the Roman Catholic Church has understood its own history. Until Vatican II at least, its understanding of its authenticity entirely rested in the idea that the authority of the popes flowed directly from Peter himself. Even Catholic scholars have pointed out that this is a shaky theory, to say the least. Even if Peter found his way to Rome, the possibility that he was made a bishop there, before such things existed, and then transmitted his office and with it his status and authority to his successors, is remote. There is also a number of occasions in the medieval period in which there were rival, or no, popes. The golden thread of apostolic authority becomes hard to retain at these moments. For all that, the sense that deliberate separation from Rome had caused all Christian division underpinned the response of the popes to ecumenism. In this, they had more of a case, at least as far as Protestants were concerned.

The Second Vatican Council, under the saintly and gracious Pope John XXIII and his ecumenically minded successor Paul VI, developed a gentler approach. While alluding to the idea of apostolic succession, the decree on ecumenism also reached deeper and further into Catholic tradition to find some common ground and a few olive branches to offer other denominations. Vitally, the document accepted Catholicism's share of the blame for past schism and, referring to other churches, affirmed that 'children ... born into these communities and who grow up believing in Christ cannot be accused of the sin involved in the separation'. It noted that Christ can be and is present beyond the Catholic Church, that baptism in other churches is valid, and urged humility, generosity and an avoidance of unnecessary argument on its Catholic readers. Significantly, it also looked to St Augustine, the fourth-century St John Chrysostom, and the previous Councils of the Church to find the seeds of some of its ideas.[4] In this time of 'updating', the Roman Catholic Church found internal resources in its own tradition, past leaders and foremost thinkers to undergird its new effort to reach out to those it had previously viewed as heretics destined for eternal punishment. In 1985, Pope John Paul II issued a much longer declaration[5] which built on the work of Vatican II, stressing the need for 'conversion' in dialogue on all sides. He looked to Pope Gregory the Great in the sixth century and to the ninth-century brothers Saints Cyril and Methodius, as well as to the earlier decrees of church councils up to and including Vatican II to illustrate his argument. Despite his generous and accommodating tone, it is interesting to detect the Pope's characteristically conservative outlook poking through the text from time to time.

Ecumenism: against tradition?

Once the Roman Catholic Church came on board, the ecumenical movement rapidly grew and flourished. The WCC, now given added authority by Catholic involvement, grew to 342 member churches in 100 countries by 2003. In its work, and in that of inter-church bodies across the world, there is always a danger of a disconnection between the detailed, complex and yet important theological pronouncements which come from their leaders, and the vast majority of Christians who attend churches week by week. They may be entirely uninterested by the ongoing consequences of the Great Schism, the Colloquy of Marburg, or the First Vatican Council, but they are often passionately concerned with expressing a common Christian identity with their neighbours. When these two levels of ecumenical engagement, the grass roots and the institutional, can be made to come together, huge progress is possible, as is the releasing of new energy and vision for mission and ministry, which, after all, was the purpose to begin with. To offer one example of personal experience, the Borough of Milton Keynes, while often (and unfairly) reviled and derided for its hideous 1960s architecture, concrete cows and 'soulless' housing estates, has from its inception been privileged with the full co-operation of the city's churches. In areas of new building, they have formed six 'Ecumenical Parishes' in which one building serves all the churches, often in united congregations. In pre-existing towns engulfed by the new city, ecumenical covenants bind the churches closely together. There are as few separate denominational meetings as possible, and one Ecumenical Moderator for the whole borough, who acts as a kind of bishop for all the churches. Currently, the Moderator is a Baptist woman pastor, the universal acceptance of whose leadership is a joyous sign of progress towards visible unity.

Places like Milton Keynes also illustrate the dangers of ecumenism, not the least of which are some traits we examined at the beginning of Chapter 1. Many Christians of good intent and great integrity have come to see any vestige of denominational identity as a backwards step, and an affront to the whole endeavour of ecumenical integration. It's certainly true, as we have already noted, that sometimes Christians cling to things which they term 'tradition' but which are really something more petty: individual cups for communion wine and jumble sales in the autumn. Claiming these things as essential to authentic Christian life in any denomination is ridiculous, and gives us all a bad name. It gives rise to the feeling, expressed by Kenneth Cracknell, that in fact we worship with those of different faiths every Sunday in church. Partly as a sensible reaction against this kind of narrowness, and partly because of an ecumenism that sees the wood but misses the trees, many Christians in ecumenical settings and projects have grown uncomfortable about espousing any ideas or approaches they think are special to their inherited way of practising the faith. To do so looks narrow, or intolerant, or just plain arrogant. It seems to undo the work of the last 40 years. And so, the prevailing wisdom goes, we resist anything that sounds like a claim to uniqueness, because 'we're all just Christians'.

The intention behind this is certainly good. The end result may, however, fall into the category of what the Second Vatican Council loftily termed 'superficiality and imprudent zeal'. For, in saying nothing which cannot be said by all, the churches and the Christians within them are in danger of adopting the 'lowest common denominator' approach, in which great treasures of the tradition – indeed, of all the traditions of the faith – are lost. A better model for the ecumenical movement is the gospel idea of a great global feast, in which everyone brings to the table some special delicacy of their own. The result is rich and varied, but still recognizably a feast, at which all are enriched by being exposed to foods which they would otherwise not have tasted. It takes some confidence, sharing with strangers that which is precious to you: but it's usually worth it. It's certainly better than a banquet to which everyone brings plain rice, lest someone else be offended by their individuality and the imposition of their personal tastes and preferences. If the last image seems ludicrous, it is the danger of an ecumenism in which tradition and denominational identity are not cherished, even as Christians grow and work more closely together. All of us have heard the kinds of sermons in which the preacher is either unwilling or unable to say anything distinctive or compelling, perhaps through fear of upsetting the congregation. The results are not usually interesting, edifying or converting; nor would such a Church be.

The other great tragedy of losing our traditional understandings about God in an ecumenical 'soup' is that we lose many of the resources which would help us to 'do' ecumenism better and more insightfully. Even if our separate denominational histories usually point towards a record of deeper divisions and endless fragmentation within the Church, they also contain, beneath the surface, all kinds of insights and treasures without which the ecumenical enterprise is the poorer. From the early days of the Church, some theologians have encouraged Christians to be attentive to the unlikely places, on the edges and at the fringes of what they consider normality, where God's Spirit is yet clearly at work. One example of this kind of thinker was the first-century theologian Justin Martyr, who wanted in his

Christian theology to acknowledge and build upon the Greek philosophical tradition which continued to shape and underpin his thought. Justin thus likened the Spirit to seed, which as it is cast often lands and grows in unusual spots. Pioneers of inter-religious dialogue have used these ideas too, as we shall see. In ecumenical work, it's an idea that moves us beyond strict definitions of Church which rest too heavily on tracing a line of authority, and towards one which looks rather at the fruit of others' hearts and lives.

Many of the religious movements which arose after the Protestant Reformation have tended to emphasize the individual's experience of God in discerning the authenticity of their faith. They make a person's life and integrity the greatest test of their religion, and not their membership (or not) of a particular group or church. George Fox in the seventeenth century drew around him a group of people who were above all interested in seeking God together, and pursuing God's will. They were not so concerned with liturgy, or doctrine, or setting any kind of boundaries around who could be deemed Christian. The intense personal experience of God which many of Fox's earliest followers underwent sometimes manifested in fits of shaking or convulsion; they were thus quickly dubbed the 'Quakers'. The name stuck. From the outset, Quakers have been known as those with a remarkable generosity of spirit and a quite unusual breadth of view. Their *Chief Principles*, drawn up in 1678 by Fox's disciple Robert Barclay, clearly stated that Christ had 'tasted death for every man; not only for some kinds of men, as some vainly talk'; and asserted that 'all true and acceptable worship to God is offered in the inward and immediate moving and drawing of His own Spirit, which is neither limited to places, times, or persons'.[6] Many contemporary devotees of the eleven o'clock Sunday morning service would still struggle with this revolutionary thought.

The influence of the Quaker ethos and its ecumenical spirit was in time exported to the New World, where it was similarly radical. The early colonies in the Americas had been founded as strictly confessional zones: Virginia for the Anglicans, Maryland for Catholics, and Massachusetts for Congregationalists, the so-called 'Puritans', whose rigour about keeping the colony's faith pure led to the execution of Quakers and the infamous Salem witch trials of 1692. The latitude and tolerance of the Founding Fathers of the USA were still a long way off. One man challenged this pattern, by buying and then expanding a Quaker settlement, which was built on his principles of religious freedom and toleration of diversity. William Penn's experiment eventually attracted all kinds of minorities, even Jews and Catholics, from Europe. He established cordial relations with the native Americans, so despised by the Puritans, and made every effort to ensure their fair treatment and give them equal access to legal redress. Penn founded a great city dedicated to his religious and social ideals and named appropriately: the city of 'brotherly love', Philadelphia. Modern Pennsylvania remains a tribute to his courage, integrity and dignity. His verdict on the sections of the Christian Church which insisted on purity to the extent that they vented and fumed against others who claimed the same faith was that they were 'unreligiously religious'; 'O God,' he prayed, 'help us not to despise or oppose what we do not understand.'[7]

William Penn lived amidst an intellectual climate which was shortly to revolutionize both Europe and the colonies. The eighteenth-century 'Enlightenment' proved a challenge to traditional forms of Christianity by its firm insistence on the supremacy of human reason, and its consequent distrust of the supernatural or miraculous, which were judged primitive when compared with rational thought. The religious expression of the Enlightenment mindset was called Deism. Its adherents pared down faith statements to a bare and quite personal minimum: Thomas Jefferson, for example, went through his New Testament excising the passages he didn't think could be true, until he was left with a collection of pieces of good advice and a Jesus who would be helpful in a crisis but would make no claims to uniqueness, still less divinity. Partly because of this conviction about the dignity of individual conscience and thought, the Deists also firmly believed in religious toleration. Jefferson, George Washington, Benjamin Franklin, James Madison and others, the founders of the modern USA, all adopted Deism, and their beliefs are reflected in the American Constitution, and in what Jefferson called 'the wall of separation between Church and State' which they made it their purpose to build.[8]

Alongside such men, others reacted to the Enlightenment with equal respect and fascination but without losing their commitment to traditional Christian belief. John Wesley's ever contradictory and intriguing belief system included a real deference to Enlightenment philosophy and learning, but no diminution of his Christian orthodoxy. He did, however, articulate quite radical ideas about the attitude due to those of different beliefs, and these continue to impact and influence Christians today. Methodism was, of course, originally a movement of Anglicans, and was always intended to remain a 'society' within the churches and not perpetuate further division. As the 'class' meetings grew and became more visible, they proved highly attractive to many, and non-Anglicans joined their numbers, including many kinds of non-Conformists: Presbyterians, Baptists and even some Catholics. Wesley himself was often accused by his opponents of the 'heresy' of many of these groups. To some 'high-church' Anglicans, he was an 'enthusiast', whose religious fervour was dangerous and destructive; by the evangelicals, he was often called 'Jesuitical', a false prophet who undermined the primacy of faith with his insistence on Christian charity. In fact, he sought only to create and foster a deepening Christian commitment which held itself accountable to other believers through prayer and weekly discussion. He was increasingly less concerned with the precise affiliation of class members, as he witnessed what he sensed was the Spirit's work in his movement, attracting a variety of followers. It was not that he didn't know what he believed, nor care what others thought: Wesley can in fact strike the modern reader as quite dictatorial and even arrogant in his religious certainty. Rather, he was given the grace not to regard differences in the brand of Christianity which Methodists professed as critical to the movement's mission.

Wesley famously tried to put flesh on the bones of this point of view in a sermon which remains a bedrock of the ecumenical movement. It relies on an unlikely text, the meeting of two men, Jehonadab and King Jehu, in 2 Kings 10. Though very different, and with very different backgrounds and outlooks, they find a common purpose. And so they join hands in agreement and mutual respect (the precise terms and aim of their agreement are best overlooked for now!). Wesley extrapolated from this nugget of scripture a beautiful plea to his hearers to place less emphasis on rigid doctrinal tests of others, and more concern to share with them God's 'energy of love' and join hands to act justly, love mercy and bear fruit in the world for the sake of the Christian gospel. In the language of his own day, Wesley's appeal was for 'opinions', or differences of view about liturgy, ethics or interpretation, to be of secondary importance to common Christian endeavour and a shared determination to work together in faithfulness to Christ's command. Wesley was careful not to allow this to be interpreted as a laissez-faire, 'anything goes' kind of Christianity. But, if there was good to be done for God in the world, he was sure that disputes over the niceties of the Christian life shouldn't hinder it. One modern interpreter of the sermon elucidates: 'To stand firmly somewhere does not exclude the possibility of challenge, of criticism or of serious exchange. Those who stand nowhere, in fact have nothing to say'. Perhaps, though, nothing expresses Wesley's message better than his brother's hymn which closes it:

Weary of all this wordly strife,
These notions, forms, and modes, and names,
To Thee, the Way, the Truth, the Life,
Whose love my simple heart inflames,
Divinely taught, at last I fly,
With Thee and Thine to live, and die.[9]

As the nineteenth century unfolded, contributions such as Wesley's continued to provide a foundation for increased denominational co-operation, even as, after his death, the Methodist Church was eventually formed, and then itself fragmented. As the missionary movements began to realize their need of greater and deeper collaboration, and the Anglican Church of England was reminded of its liturgical and theological debt to Rome and its place in and inheritance from the wider Church by the Oxford Movement, slowly the scenery started to shift, even while the fragmentation of Christ's body seemed to be played out centre stage. When the climate changed, and all denominations gradually began to explore more deeply the scandal of their divisive history and the imperative to work and worship more closely together, resources such as Wesley's challenge to the Methodists and Fox's revolutionary inclusiveness were close at hand, just beneath the surface. And they were still startlingly relevant and timely.

Those who have been leaders in the Church's engagement of other religious groups, too, have had to answer the question: is this a totally new departure in our history? Or is there precedent and therefore authority for it? They have found some of their answers in the same places as the ecumenists. Penn's inclusion of Jews and the Native Americans in his settlements reflected a general Quaker disposition towards 'tolerance' and, beyond that, a genuine interest in and respect for diversity. Wesley's descriptions of his encounters with those of other faiths reflect the mindset of an eighteenth-century gentleman by being less than entirely positive: but his openness of mind and heart also prodded him into some more generous (and, for the time, unusual) reflections on Jews and Muslims, especially late in life.[10] Both men reveal that a 'catholic spirit' leads believers even beyond the bounds of the Church in dialogue, mutual ministry and growth. Increasingly, leaders in the churches have been tying together the need for inter-Christian reconciliation, which is widely accepted, and the urgency for interreligious conversations, which can be neglected or cause fear. As one puts it, 'the

"Christian ecumenism" and the "wider ecumenism" are not mutually exclusive', nor should we 'place greater emphasis on the one over the other'.[11]

Those who have engaged deeply in interreligious conversations, though, have sometimes gone even further in discovering theological resources in the tradition than have their colleagues in the ecumenical scene. Kenneth Cracknell in particular has written movingly of the 'Logos' theology of the early Greek Church, which was willing to recognize the presence of God's Spirit in places and people beyond the Church, moving them towards holiness and truth. In particular, as with the work of Justin Martyr, their intent was to honour and give theological respectability to the Greek philosophers whose work they so greatly admired and adopted. Clement of Alexandria (c.150–c.215) was prepared to add Buddhists to the number of those moved by the same indwelling Spirit as Christians. One of the greatest of all theologians, Athanasius (c.296–373), took these ideas further, reaffirming the life-giving Spirit of God in *all* humanity, Christian and non-Christian alike. Such authors were not really pioneers of interreligious dialogue, to be fair: but they articulated a much more gracious account of God's presence and purpose in all people than their Latin counterparts, and Cracknell's work is very important in providing this ancient, authoritative foundation for contemporary work. It reminds us that, in Clement's words, 'into [the way of truth], as into a perennial river, streams flow from all sides'. John Wesley, who greatly admired these early Greek theologians, used also to remind the Methodists to be aware of the 'prevenience' of God's grace: *all* life, in its beauty, wonder and diversity, owes its origin to the breath of God. No one, whatever their creed, is without God's presence. Would-be evangelists should remember that, no matter to whom they go, in their company they stand on holy ground: God is already there.[12]

Even amid the brutality of the Crusades, it remains possible to find flickers of the light of this kind of thought. Saint Francis of Assisi, although it seems that in general he was willing to approve of the pope's call to arms, was also capable of a more notable greatness of heart. In 1219, the story goes, he ventured past the rows of soldiers engaging in the Fifth Crusade, to speak with Sultan Malik al-Kamil and share with him something of the simple Christian faith which gave him life. By all accounts, the two men managed, even for a moment, to recognize each other as brothers; Francis was shown mercy by the Muslim leader, who even returned him home to Italy after their conversation. Perhaps, in his determination to restore the Christian faith to the simple, basic teachings and grace of Jesus, in his material poverty and openness of heart, Francis – and the Sultan with him – discovered a timeless moment of spiritual insight even among the cruelty, bigotry and violence all around them. Their encounter, and the Greek Logos theology, is reflected by the poet William Blake, who, in a poem written nearly 600 years after Francis, allowed his experience of God in the Other to speak:

> To Mercy, Pity, Peace and Love,
> All pray in their distress;
> And to these virtues of delight
> Return their thankfulness.
>
> And all must love the human form,
> In heathen, Turk or Jew;
> Where Mercy, Love and Pity dwell:
> There God is dwelling too.

These moments of generosity and grace spring from encounters between those of different faiths who are sufficiently humble and open to seeing beneath what is dissimilar to what is shared. Increasingly, as Christians from the West encountered those of other religious traditions, such insights became possible. Cracknell draws attention to figures such as the eighteenth-century Bartholomeus Ziegenbalg, the first Protestant missionary to India. Ziegenbalg, unlike so many others of his vocation, determined to immerse himself in Hindu faith, culture and life, and even became a prominent champion of the Tamil language. Although he made many converts to Christianity, his methods were never polemical, dismissive or unkind. Accounts of his life portray a truly Christian man of humble, open spirit, in whose conversations with his neighbours we find precursors of the modern interfaith movement. Ziegenbalg was followed in India by the Cambridge academic and chaplain Henry Martyn (1781–1812). Martyn annoyed his fellow Englishmen by entering respectfully, interestedly and courteously into dialogue with the Indians, and by his steadfast commitment to both mission and an openness of heart. Martyn spent time in Persia also; his short life moved and touched many in both places with its integrity and generosity.[13]

Later missionaries wrote in the same spirit as Ziegenbalg and Martyn and built on their work. Charles Freer Andrews devoted his life after ordination in 1897 to India, and spent some 34 years there. He formed deep friendships with the Hindu M. K. Gandhi and the Brahmoist Rabindranath Tagore, both highly influential figures in the move towards independence. Andrews spoke of the 'widening' which these friendships gave his Christian faith, of his 'finding new visions of Christ' in his Hindu friends, and of how he saw the same driving principles in the religion of Guru Nanak and others as in his own. 'I cannot', he reflected, 'use the word "heathen" as I used to do.' Andrews seemed to produce a whole generation of Asian 'children', native-born Christians who continued to develop his mission and theology. Lakshman Wickremesinghe was a Sri Lankan Anglican bishop who had a concern to be faithful to his Christian faith and its tradition while acknowledging the diversity of faith in Sri Lanka, and honouring what these faiths held in common. Speaking in 1982, he described his cathedral in the town of Kurunegala, the focal point of which was a huge sculpture of the crucified Christ, very much in the model of the statues of the Buddha at some shrines. Wickremesinghe noted also the Hindu elements of some of the worship in the cathedral, and what he termed 'innovation and continuity with biblical perspective'. He concluded by expressing the hope that the whole worshipping life of his cathedral would be both faithful to Christ and also demonstrate God's universal love for all humanity.[14]

These missionaries and their spiritual offspring offer timely guidance to both the ecumenical and interfaith movements. By remaining firmly rooted in their own faith traditions, and yet being gracious enough to be open in humility and trust to others, they reflect the kind of model we sketched earlier, and warn us against that kind of dialogue which seeks only to diminish ourselves and others to what can be agreed upon. It is possible to be faithful both to a tradition and to our neighbour. Martin Forward describes this as being like the difference between flowers and butterflies; in any kind of 'ecumenical' meeting, inside or beyond the Church, it is far better to be a flower, drawing sustenance from our roots and yet able to turn and face the warmth of others' suns. Butterflies spend their short lives in an endless search for something new, and rarely settle anywhere for long.[15] Sometimes, of course, our tradition needs 'updating'; when Pope Paul VI issued the Vatican II document, *Nostra Aetate*, which for the first time took seriously the harm done by Christians to those of other faiths and authorized and even required dialogue to begin, it represented a significant shift. Even so, it was not in that unfaithful to what had gone before. Christian tradition at its richest and deepest teaches us to balance rootedness with openness, confidence with humility, and the desire to bear witness with the ability to listen. Only then is true dialogue, and real transformation, possible.

Nor is this kind of thing the preserve only of theologians, bishops, the great and the good. Indeed, some of the most effective and reconciling interreligious conversations and friendships happen between lay people. As the world shrinks and our neighbours become ever more diverse, it becomes correspondingly more easy to encounter religious diversity: at the bus stop, at the school gates, in the workplace, pub, shop and fitness centre. Three extraordinary New York women met in exactly such mundane ways, and began their own 'Faith Club'. Ranya Idliby is Muslim, Suzanne Oliver Christian and Priscilla Warner Jewish. They describe how their meetings took them through difficult and dangerous terrain, in which trust and vulnerability were as hard to develop as they were to maintain; they reflect on encountering the shameful and sinful areas of their own faith history and tradition; and they also end with a glowing affirmation of Andrews' sense of the 'widening' of one's own faith commitment that comes through genuine, open relationship with people who hold another. They were enabled through dialogue 'to recognize that there is truth within [other faiths] without feeling threatened by that recognition'. Their holy experiment is a challenge to us all.[16]

'A New Earth'? The dangers of being rootless

It is perhaps worth considering more than cursorily what happens, and what the dangers might be, of the kind of spirituality which rejects any tradition, and forgoes rootedness in any one time-honoured, tried-and-tested religious framework. To recall Martin Forward's image, we should examine the dangers of being a butterfly. The varied spiritualities of the so-called 'New Age' movement exemplify this phenomenon best. Chief among them nowadays is the German spiritual writer and teacher, Eckhart Tolle; his work offers an opportunity for such a study, and is worth some detailed attention. Tolle's books, especially *The Power of Now*, and its sequel *A New Earth*, have gained huge international popularity, on the forging of which he has become a multimillionaire.[17] While acknowledging some indebtedness to a considerable number of religious influences, Tolle simultaneously advocates the rejection of them. He chose his own first name in his youth because of his Catholic upbringing and his admiration for the medieval Christian mystic Meister Eckhart, whom we encountered earlier. However, Tolle experienced what he terms a spiritual 'catharsis' aged 29, and found himself challenged and impacted by the practice of Zen Buddhism. While his evolving philosophy clearly owes something also to Taoism, to other forms of Buddhist practice, and to a residual Christian affection for some parts of the New Testament, the resulting teaching is uniquely and distinctly his own, and is very well tailored to appeal to and massage the prevailing desires and tendencies of the early twenty-first century.

Tolle's teaching rests on a rejection of the famous dictum of the Enlightenment thinker René Descartes: 'I think, therefore I am'. He claims that it is thought in fact which clouds our minds, prevents us from encountering true reality, and damagingly affects our understanding of our deepest selves. The constant stream of our thinking actually prevents us from attaining the true enlightenment: the ability to live wholly, peacefully and contentedly in the present, the 'now' of his book's title. The past, he warns, is inaccessible, because it is past and should therefore be forgotten. All thoughts of the future are only signs of our wanting, indications of our sense of lacking something, and clear evidence of our innate dissatisfaction with who we are. Therefore, the only way to contentment, to peace, is an ability to live entirely in the present moment, without reference to either past or future. Our emotions, too, Tolle adds, are merely the 'body's reaction to the mind', and are therefore as valueless as our thought streams.

The way to overcome thought and emotion, in Tolle's view, is to refuse to derive any sense of who we are from what he calls the 'content', or sometimes the 'form', of life. By this, he means any exterior identity by which we choose to define ourselves: nationality, politics, possessions, fears, dislikes, even religious affiliation. All of these, he claims, are impermanent; they offer no real sense of reality. Instead, he advocates the creation of 'inner space', free of all attachments and commitments, and in that to find freedom and a unique individual understanding of self. Needless to say, Tolle has formulated a number of methods and techniques to enable his readers to establish this level of detachment from all that otherwise normally characterizes human life and society. Not only does he regard religion as unhelpful here, but also he stresses the need to be entirely amnesiac about the past, because of our tendency to interpret the present in the light of it. 'Your conditioned mind', he cautions, 'is the result of all your past history as well as of the collective cultural mindset you inherited. So you see and judge the present through the eyes of the past and get a totally distorted view of it.'[18]

Not surprisingly, Tolle has little need for, and a great caution surrounding, God. He believes in what he calls 'one formless and eternal Life', which is the same as our own essence, and the essence of all beings. 'In other words,' as he puts it, 'everywhere you encounter yourself.' If this were not a frightening enough thought, he finds that the word 'God' has become so conditioned by myriad historical and cultural associations that it should rarely, if ever, be used. Instead, he prefers to encourage his followers towards a more interiorized sense of Presence, which the individual encounters and experiences in unique ways, presumably somewhat resembling the individual concerned. As he advises, in a statement which reveals both a debt to traditional religious teaching and a desire to discourage its further propagation: 'instead of quoting the Buddha, be the Buddha, be "the awakened one"'. Asked by a reader of his website about the value of the New Testament, Tolle opts again for his characteristically subjective approach. It contains truth, he thinks, but also grave misrepresentations and untruths, perpetrated by those wanting to use the figure of Jesus for their own ends and purposes. How to know the one from the other? Detachment, and a cultivation of his methods of centring on the 'now'; in this state of being, freed from the addiction of thought and the distortion of past and culture, one can 'access [one's] inner knowing', and have clear knowledge. One wonders whether the world's New Testament scholars could simply bypass the research process through access to Tolle's meditative practices.[19]

In fairness, Tolle does describe some positive effects of his work and advice. He agrees with most world faiths that the cultivation of love is the goal of all this, though not the kind of love he terms 'egoic', for instance the kind that is anxious about a loved one leaving or ceasing to love in return. Asked about a possible conflict between his desire for love, joy and peace in the individual and his aversion to emotions, he responds that

> love, joy and peace are deep states of Being or rather three aspects of the state of inner connectedness with Being. As such they have no opposite. Emotions, on the other hand, being part of the dualistic mind, are subject to the law of opposites.

Even disregarding the reality of hate, despair and conflict in human experience, we can see in this philosophy some considerable redefinition of what religions have usually meant by those words and ideals.

It is not difficult to see why such teaching has become so attractive to so many. Asked about the apparent contradiction between his insistence upon 'detachment' from 'form' and 'content' and his extraordinary worldwide selling-power and consequent wealth creation, Tolle replies that he merely responds to the demand, does nothing to create it and is thus entirely free from the false emotion of greed. There are deeper and darker problems with his thought, however. For all the occasional echoes in his writing of some aspects of some religions, all of them almost as one accuse him, from the deep wells of tradition, of neglecting and even denying some of their most powerful and transformative elements. Most of them would ask what room there is in his practice for openness to a transcendent reality beyond ourselves, which questions, challenges and convicts us, and draws us out of patterns of selfishness, ignorance and injustice to a better, fuller life. From a Christian perspective, several reflections arise. If yearning for a different future is merely a destructive attachment to dissatisfaction and the 'addiction' of thought, what room is left for

William Wilberforce's campaign to end slavery, or Elizabeth
Fry's fight for better conditions for prisoners, or Martin Luther
King's great dream of a day when his children would be free
from segregation? What openness can there ever be to the loving purposes of a God who desires healing and salvation for
a divided and broken world? What room is there for a God
who gently calls us to acknowledge our own contribution to
humanity's mess before receiving forgiveness and the chance
of a truly 'new birth', which indeed liberates us from destructive patterns of thought and action? What of the great biblical
promise of renewed human community? In place of the great
ambitious scope of the Christian faith at its fullest, noblest and
most optimistic, Tolle offers an entirely subjective, rootless
guide to self-satisfied disengagement with the world. It is, as
the New Testament scholar John Dominic Crossan observes,
'ME-ditation'. It comes also entirely tailored to the predilections of the wealthy West; it is hard to imagine *The Power of
Now* being useful, insightful or remotely relevant to the refugee
camps of Darfur, the feeding stations of Ethiopia, the lines of
the unemployed in Zimbabwe or the death camps of North
Korea.

Sometimes, a long faith tradition which cherishes the voices
of those who have sought God over many centuries also helpfully enables us to recognize something for what it is. Tolle's
worldview resembles nothing so much as a contemporary form
of an ancient heresy. In the early days of the Church, many
Christian thinkers and Church leaders found themselves battling a series of philosophies known collectively as Gnosticism.
Saint Augustine himself was a member of one such sect, the
Manichees, in his early life, and his conversion to and formation in Christianity was profoundly shaped by his rejection of
their thought. Gnostics, broadly speaking, thought that to at-
tain spiritual insight one must first possess a 'secret' knowledge,
method or way of thinking, which is not innate or obvious
and so needs to be shared and mastered. They believed that
they were thus in possession of spiritual treasure which marked

them out from the mass of humanity, and their philosophy centred on the absolute imperative to seek this kind of individual achievement. They usually stressed detachment and a retreat from the material world in all its messiness, in favour of an interiorized form of faith. They almost always looked to a particular spiritual guru or guide, whom they sought to emulate along the path to this hidden holiness, but who commonly turned out not to have all the answers to which they laid claim. Their idea of the divine was of a remote, unknowable, unrevealed higher being who cannot be spoken of with accuracy and bears virtually no relation to the God of Judaeo-Christian faith as revealed in the Bible. That lesser God they called the 'demiurge', or 'craftsman', because of his willingness to deal in sordid matters such as the created order and human affairs.

Parallels with Tolle's thought are many and obvious: the obsession with self, the distrust of matter and creation, the way in which Tolle himself assumes the role of guide and guru. Christians have rejected Gnostic views for a number of reasons: God made the material world to be good, and to be the forum in which salvation can be worked out; the good news of God's love in Christ is not a closed secret, but an open invitation to the poor, the downtrodden and all who know their need of Grace; Christians are to be Christ's representatives, in and of the world, and not those who reject human community and the wellsprings of their tradition's wisdom in order to pursue an entirely subjective personal advancement. As we choose the influences on our own spiritual lives, the wisdom of Christian tradition would still seem to warn us away from those whom Jesus called 'false messiahs and false prophets', and 'blind guides'.[20]

Keble and Mohammed: conversion and experience

Pope John Paul II's encyclical on ecumenism talks frequently about the need for 'conversion'. By this, he does not mean that those engaged in dialogue should change their religious commitments, or make a move from Anglicanism to Catholicism, or from Islam to Christianity. Certainly, this happens sometimes in respectful and open friendship between denominations and faiths. It isn't, however, the main purpose. The kind of conversion he talks about is more subtle, a shift in heart and soul away from exclusivism and intolerance towards openness, mutual exchange and even transformation through encounter with those who are different from us. Whenever people of faith move away from their need always and incontrovertibly to be right, from their ivory towers of complacency and certitude, and open themselves to dialogue and the exchange of gifts, they find their faith enriched. Interestingly, too, they usually find themselves strengthened and renewed in their existing faith commitment and tradition. They return to the 'rootedness' of where they come from with a new, deeper and stronger understanding of it. Mysteriously, yet invariably, dialogue opens us up to the holy ground of the place from which we started.

Perhaps this is best illustrated, encountered and understood through personal experience. For me, two significant exposures, one to Christian diversity and the other to another faith, shaped and strengthened my commitment to Methodist Christianity. Arriving at university aged 19, I was fortunate to be a member of college in which there was a strong worshipping community in the college chapel and a very effective chaplain, who made a point of cultivating wide ownership of chapel life and liturgy. The college had been founded in memory of a Victorian saint, John Keble, one of the leaders of the nineteenth-century Oxford Movement, and therefore had a definite 'high church' tradition. The Sunday eucharist was formal; the clergy wore full vestments; the service always made much use of choral elements, and even occasionally availed itself of incense. Coming from a rather 'low church' background, I was initially rather intimidated by all this loftiness and grandeur: and then quickly found myself in a love affair with it. I became heavily involved in chapel life, and it gave me, beyond community, life and breath and quite urgent reminders about God. I was, in worship, in the presence of that which is greater than I, incomprehensible, unknowable, worthy of awe and evincing wonder from the worshipper. I simply needed to be brought back to the simple but humbling observation that God is bigger than my sense of God. In music, poetry, liturgy and even formality, I experienced conversion. Not that I became an Anglican, despite a momentary crisis about whether to do so. The chaplain, by then a bishop, sensed that I needed to return to my Methodist roots with this new 'widening' of my faith. He was right, and I continue to cherish all that those years taught and revealed to me.

Six years later, in my first year at theological college, I was sent to Cape Town, South Africa, for a month. I worked mainly with Methodist churches, except for three days spent with one of the city's imams. Rashied Omar was then at the Claremont Road mosque, and it and he were centres of renewal in the city's Muslim population. Rashied's deep commitment to dialogue had led to the mosque becoming an unusual kind of place, encouraging gender equality and welcoming a range of preachers from beyond Islam. Above all, Rashied had been a fearless prophet in South Africa's long struggle for freedom and justice. He worked tirelessly with other faith leaders to bring about the transition to true democracy and oversee fair elections. He had lasting friendships, with Archbishops Desmond Tutu and Njongonkulu Ndungane among others. It was an extraordinary privilege to see this aspect of his ministry, to listen to him talk about the dangers, joys, exasperations and ultimate triumph of the fight for peace, in God's name. I was converted: not to Islam, but to a renewed understanding of the forces of goodness, truth and joy which religious faith can unleash in the world. In a final conversation which I shall never forget, I tried to explain to him that I would return home determined to be a better Christian because of the qualities I had seen in him and his life. With amazing generosity and breathtaking grace, he returned the compliment.

Such experiences as these are not uncommon. They come

to any who are willing to lay aside prejudice, intolerance and fear, however reluctantly and uncertainly, and be open to encounter with another. They are the experiences, not just of liberal twentieth-century Christians, but of all those, from Jesus onwards, who have continued a noble tradition of inclusivity, grace and welcome in their faith. The ecumenical and inter-religious movements are not 'doing a new thing'. They are mining the brightest and best in their faith history and walking in the footsteps of saints and pioneers who went before them. The tension with more fundamentalist versions of faith will always be present, for all faiths. For us Christians, and our household, we must hold true to the essential lessons of our history. As one writer on spirituality puts it:

If the love of truth and the love of God is also love for those who suffer and struggle toward a vision of the reconciliation of all things in God, then there remains a bright promise. This is the hope for a more inclusive Christian life for the sake of the whole inhabited world.[21]

The future of our faith, as its past, rests in such a vision.

Notes

1 Martin Forward tells this story in his book *Inter-Religious Dialogue: A Short Introduction*, Oxford: Oneworld, 2001, p. 32.

2 Report of the Central Committee of the WCC meeting in Rolle, Switzerland, 1951, quoted by Dr Mary Cotes in an unpublished lecture.

3 John 17.21.

4 *Unitatis Redintegratio* ('The Restoration of Unity'), published in 1964, and available at <www.vatican.va/archive>.

5 *Ut Unum Sint* ('That they may be one'), again, a reference to John 17.21 (document also at Vatican website).

6 Quoted in Henry Bettenson and Chris Maunder (eds), *Documents of the Christian Church*, Oxford: Oxford University Press, 1999, pp. 339–40.

7 Unreferenced, but commonly attributed to Penn.

8 Jefferson coined the phrase in an 1802 letter to Baptists in Danbury, Massachusetts. Nowhere in the First Amendment to the US Constitution, which guaranteed freedom of religious expression and forbade the establishment of religion in the country, is the phrase used.

9 Robert Gribben, 'The Catholic Spirit', in Angela Shier-Jones and Kim Dunnam Reisman (eds), *44 Sermons to Serve the Present Age*, Peterborough: Epworth Press, 2007, pp. 213–14; John Wesley, *John Wesley's 44 Sermons*, London: Epworth Press, 1988, p. 455.

10 For an account of these, see, for example, Martin Forward's summary in *Inter-Religious Dialogue* pp. 47–54.

11 S. Wesley Ariarajah, 'A Future That May Be Greater than Its Past', in Martin Forward, Stephen Plant and Susan White (eds), *A Great Commission*, Bern: Peter Lang, 2000, pp. 169–86.

12 Kenneth Cracknell, *In Good and Generous Faith*, Peterborough: Epworth Press, 2005, pp. 47–54. The Clement quotation is from his *Stromateis*, 1.5.1–3.

13 Cracknell, *In Good and Generous Faith*, pp. 165–9.

14 Quoted in Geoffrey Rowell, Kenneth Stevenson and Rowan Williams (eds), *Love's Redeeming Work*, Oxford: Oxford University Press, 2001, p. 555, from Charles Freer Andrews' 'A Missionary's Experience' (in *The Indian Interpreter*, Poona, 1909) and p. 739, from a paper written by Lackshman Wickremesinghe in 1982.

15 Forward, *Inter-Religious Dialogue*, p. 3.

16 Ranya Idliby, Suzanne Oliver and Priscilla Warner, *The Faith Club*, New York: Free Press, 2007, p. 308.

17 Eckhart Tolle, *The Power of Now*, Novato: New World Library, 1999, and *A New Earth*, New York: Penguin, 2008.

18 A quotation from Tolle's *The Power of Now*, reprinted on the Tolle fansite, <www.innergrowth.info>.

19 Tolle's own website, <eckharttolle.com>, contains this and other answers to readers' questions. The wonderful US public radio programme on religious matters, *Speaking of Faith*, also has an informative website on which there is a full, hour-long interview with Tolle about his thought and spirituality.

20 Mark 13.22; Matthew 23.16.

21 Don Saliers, 'Christian Spirituality in an Ecumenical Age', in L. Dupré and D. Saliers (eds), *Christian Spirituality: Post-Reformation and Modern*, New York: Crossroad, 1989, pp. 520–44.

EPILOGUE

Heart in Pilgrimage

The road to the village takes you off the dual carriageway, through Leighton Bromswold, whose parish church once boasted George Herbert as its vicar, and out into the Cambridgeshire countryside. This far west of Cambridge and the Fens, the landscape undulates gently, a mixture of pastures, arable fields and tiny isolated settlements. The road narrows the further on one goes, until finally it becomes a simple track, with a raised grass verge running down the middle which brushes against the underside of the car. At the end is a simple farmhouse and a tiny church, without tower or ornament, in front of which there is a plain tomb. As the traveller leaves the car, he or she encounters an almost perfect peace, punctuated only by the cry of a woodland bird or the hum of a distant tractor. It feels like holy ground. And it is.

The tomb is that of Nicholas Ferrar. In 1626, he moved his family here to begin an experiment in Christian community. They came to this deserted spot and adopted the tiny church for their life of prayer, committing that, at any particular moment, there should be someone praying within it. Though their life provoked criticism from those thinking it too monastic for the reformed Church of England, they never adopted any Rule or took any vows of obligation, beyond the obligation they had to God and to one another. For many, their life was an inspiration,

163

an exercise in dedication, holiness and prayerful renewal. Their retreat from their previous wealth and influence in order simply to pursue a religious vocation together was virtually unprecedented. They were even visited by the king. Among those friends and admirers too was George Herbert, by now a priest outside Salisbury, who, as he lay dying, sent the manuscripts of his poetry to Ferrar. Their subsequent publication under Ferrar's patronage offered to the world a collection as well regarded then, and as profound, as they continue to be now.

Pilgrims can examine, in the farmhouse which doubles as a museum, the guest book from the church. There, on the page for 1936, they may see the signature of the most celebrated visitor, the poet T. S. Eliot. He was captivated by his experience there, and named one of his finest and best-known poems after the place: Little Gidding. The poem is a characteristically complex and difficult reflection on history, faith, past and present, love, life and death. Eliot found himself overwhelmed by the sheer sacredness of the place, by its air of purity and prayerfulness, and sensed himself on holy ground which needed above all not to be analysed or dispassionately described, but revered:

> You are not here to verify,
> Instruct yourself, or inform curiosity
> Or carry report. You are here to kneel
> Where prayer has been valid.[1]

In our tendency to judge ourselves as superior, in knowledge, skills and science, to the generations which came before us, places like Little Gidding break through our complacency and arrogance, and teach us to remove our shoes, to kneel, to acknowledge the presence of God in the lives of those far-distant ancestors, and to be humbled.

There are many places like this. Chapter 1 described Ely Cathedral, and its silent but constant testimony to prayer, both corporate and individual, to the turbulence of previous ages, and to the constancy of faith, hope and love. The Scottish minister George MacLeod talked of the island of Iona as a place in which the veil between earth and heaven is 'as thin as gossamer', because he felt it to be another. Iona has a 'thinness', and heaven feels closer there, in part because of its history. From Saint Columba's arrival here in 563, through the construction of an abbey, and the maintenance of a monastic community, to the present-day Iona Community founded by MacLeod which exercises a global ministry, the island has been a place 'where prayer has been valid', a centre of worship, contemplation, evangelization, protest and discipline. It bears witness to history, but to a history which continues directly to inform and inspire the present. The thousands of pilgrims who flock to this remote windswept island every year come because it is a spot in which the past meets the present, where ancient wisdom blends with a modern seeking after God, a place in which life, and faith, and the task of Christian disciples seem somehow constant and timeless.

In our exploration through the last several chapters, it has been a central theme of the argument that, as Christians, we have a history which speaks to us in this kind of way. That is, we are able to find wisdom, resources and guidance for our contemporary Christian lives, not just in places which resonate with the past, but from that past itself. As we encounter Augustine, Francis, Luther, Wesley, Keble, John XXIII and the rest, we are not asked to lose our critical faculties or blindly to accept everything they ever said and did as gospel for us too: far from it. But we are required first 'to kneel where prayer has been valid', to acknowledge their striving and seeking after God in their own time, and to honour their discoveries, their struggles, their intent, their faith. In their lives, in the lives of all those who came before us and who sought, however imperfectly, to pursue faithfulness, integrity and truth, there are always 'thin' places, in which something of the human condition and God's loving responses to it may become clearer to us. It may be that we merely learn from their mistakes; but equally, it may turn out that we find ourselves converted.

We know enough to know that sometimes it takes a little work before the veil is drawn back or the lessons of the past reveal themselves to us. It takes time and a new perspective to see our forebears in faith, not as strange figures from a distant land, but as sisters and brothers on the pilgrimage of faith. We are so often discouraged by the sheer unfamiliarity and dissimilarity of their lives and cultures, their environment and situation, that we think the effort too great. And so we need a model, a set of tools to help us mine the meaning of their lives and their times, in all their glory and tragedy, triumph and disaster, honour and shame. Just as effective preachers employ a set of tools in interpreting and understanding the ancient and unfamiliar texts and locations of the Bible, so too must we exercise care, attention and diligence in trying to understand and benefit from our rich legacy of faith. Indeed, the need to wrestle with our inheritance in this kind of way is no less urgent than the need to be in constant dialogue with our foundational scriptures. The result shapes and moulds the kind of people – and the kind of believers – we are. It offers answers to the most basic questions about us – and our God. Historical theology is theology, to state the obvious: and so how we explore what we have received from those who went before us also defines the kind of God we worship and the kind of believers we become.

There are always dangers, of course. There is the danger of neglecting this entirely, becoming the amnesiacs we met earlier, who dismiss the need for rootedness, trust their own sense of God, and eschew all earlier roadmaps in favour of a subjective inner compass of their own. They end up failing to find the field in which the treasure they seek lies buried. Then, there are those who view tradition not as a spiritual guide, but as a book of the strictest rules. What has been received must be followed to the letter, they believe, and previous generations speak with such an authoritative voice that we are not free to alter in any respect their faith nor the way they practised it. These historical fundamentalists, like all fundamentalists, will find it imposible to engage with modernity in any way that is gracious, compassionate or responsive: and will thus in their own way deny the core of the faith they claim, and the extraordinary vision of the man at its centre. Those who are willing to do the work, to deal with what is unfamiliar, unsettling or downright offensive, to overcome dissimilarity and peel away the layers of distance between the past and the present, those who hold to the difficult middle way between these two extremes, will find the treasure. They will discover the breadth and depth of their inheritance of faith; they will glimpse its possibilities and potential, and enter a 'thin' place in which God still speaks, down the ages and across them, to the consuming passions and problems of the human race. They are the ones slowly being released into fullness of life, a life shared not just with their neighbours, but with the great cloud of witnesses who accompany them on their way. As Eliot wrote after visiting Little Gidding:

> History may be servitude,
> History may be freedom.

There is, finally, no one interpretation of the tradition we share which is true. There is no hidden code which will unlock all its meaning for those privileged to share it, no Gnostic secret waiting to be revealed. There is only the discipline of prayer, of study, of thought, conversation and experience. There is also, of course, the presence of God's Spirit, who breathes through this age as every age, convicting, challenging, renewing and leading onward. When human beings have been alive and attentive to that Spirit, the Spirit of Jesus, they have seen – and been able to aspire to – all that is best, fullest and most free in their living. They have sensed God's ambitious dream for the world, and participated in unbinding their own age from its sin, failure and false desire. Following in their footsteps, we still share their task, and declare to the world the breathtaking grace and goodness of our God.

Amidst all the perplexing dissimilarity of the lives of our ancestors, all our struggles to understand their lives and actions

and faith, in our sorrow at their sin and our joy in their la-
bours, it may yet be possible to point to continuity. It is the
perpetual human need and search for a sign of God's presence
and a sense of God's character. In the Christian tradition, when
God has been apprehended and glimpsed, however fleetingly,
the experience has inspired some of the finest creative activity
in humanity's knowledge and history. We have had a sight at
such moments of all we can be and the glory of the vision to
which we are called. In Jesus, of course, that glimpse is clear-
est and that knowledge fullest. Ever since Paul wrote to the
Christians in Corinth about the virtue which comes before all
others, the tradition about Jesus, what he shows us of God and
what he makes possible for us all in every time and place, has
acquired a certain consistency and continuity in the lives of his
followers. 'He who is filled with love', Augustine claimed, 'is
filled with God.' Nine centuries later, Mother Julian agreed,
defining the message of Jesus succinctly: 'Love', she assured,
'is his meaning.' The Methodist contribution to the Christian
story rested on the Wesleys' firm conviction:

Jesu, thou art all compassion,
Pure unbounded Love thou art.

'The love which we bear for others', Brother Roger of Taizé
similarly concluded in recent decades, 'remains the mark of the
authenticity of our contemplation.'[2] Let these act as representative spokespeople: we could highlight hundreds more.

Perhaps, in this vision of God in Christ, of extraordinary
welcome, radical hospitality and infinite, endless mercy, we
come closest to a message which may be said to be timeless. It
summons us towards grace, and simultaneously sends us out
into God's world in God's name to incarnate God's loving,
tender regard for all humanity in lives of passion, peace, justice
and joy. In such a task, we surely find ourselves in the company
of the saints. Perhaps no one has ever managed to express it
more luminously than Nicholas Ferrar's friend George Her-

bert, writing 400 years ago, after wars, persecution and hatred had divided families and nations and devastated the Church. God calls us, and the whole inhabited earth along with us, to overcome the fears which bind us and our habitual capacity for self-destruction, and discover our truest selves, held now and for eternity in the firm embrace of divine love:

> Love bade me welcome, yet my soul drew back,
> Guilty of dust and sin.
> But quick-ey'd Love, observing me grow slack
> From my first entrance in,
> Drew nearer to me, sweetly questioning
> If I lack'd anything.
>
> 'A guest,' I answer'd, 'worthy to be here';
> Love said, 'You shall be he.'
> 'I, the unkind, the ungrateful? ah my dear,
> I cannot look on thee.'
> Love took my hand and smiling did reply,
> 'Who made the eyes but I?'
>
> 'Truth, Lord, but I have marr'd them; let my shame
> Go where it doth deserve.'
> 'And know you not,' says Love, 'who bore the blame?'
> 'My dear, then I will serve.'
> 'You must sit down,' says Love, 'and taste my meat.'
> So I did sit and eat.[3]

Notes

1 T. S. Eliot, *Four Quartets*, London: Faber, 1944 (2001), p. 36.

2 Quoted by Hannah Ward and Jennifer Wild in *Christian Quotation Collection*, Oxford: Lion, 1997, p. 303 (no reference given).

3 George Herbert (ed. John Tobin), *The Complete English Poems*, London: Penguin, 1991, p. 178.

ACKNOWLEDGEMENT OF SOURCES

T. S. Eliot, 'Little Gidding', from the *Four Quartets*, Faber and Faber, 1944 (2001).

Andrew Motion, 'Remember This: An Elegy on the Death of HM Queen Elizabeth The Queen Mother', from *Public Property*, Faber and Faber, 2002.

Brian Wren, 'Deep in the shadows of the past' © 1975, 1995 Stainer & Bell Ltd, London, England, <www.stainer.co.uk> for the world excluding USA, Canada, Australia and New Zealand, which are controlled by Hope Publishing Company, USA, <www.hopepublishing.com>. Reprinted by permission of Stainer & Bell.

Wendell Berry, 'At a Country Funeral', *Selected Poems of Wendell Berry* © 1999, Counterpoint. Reprinted by permission of Counterpoint.